Dynamic THINKING

THE TECHNIQUE for ACHIEVING SELF-CONFIDENCE and SUCCESS

by

Melvin Powers

1979 Edition

Published by
Melvin Powers
WILSHIRE BOOK COMPANY
12015 Sherman Road
No. Hollywood, California 91605
Telephone: (213) 875-1711

Printed by

HAL LEIGHTON PRINTING COMPANY
P.O. Box 3952
North Hollywood, California 91605
Telephone: (213) 983-1105

Printed in the United States of America

Library of Congress Catalog Card Number: 54-13486

ISBN 0-87980-031-3

CONTENTS

IT COULDN'T BE DONE

by EDGAR A. GUEST

Somebody said that it couldn't be done,
　　But he with a chuckle replied
That "maybe it couldn't," but he would be one
　　Who wouldn't say so till he tried.
So he buckled right in with the trace of a grin
　　On his face. If he worried he hid it.
He started to sing as he tackled the thing
　　That couldn't be done, and he did it.

Somebody scoffed: "Oh, you'll never do that,
　　At least no one ever has done it;"
But he took off his coat and he took off his hat,
　　And the first thing we knew he'd begun it,
With a lift of his chin and a bit of a grin,
　　Without any doubting or quiddit,
He started to sing as he tackled the thing
　　That couldn't be done, and he did it.

There are thousands to tell you it cannot be done,
　　There are thousands to prophesy failure;
There are thousands to point out to you, one by one,
　　The dangers that wait to assail you.
But just buckle in with a bit of a grin,
　　Just take off your coat and go to it;
Just start to sing as you tackle the thing
　　That "cannot be done," and you'll do it.

FOREWORD

IT IS HOPED THAT THIS BOOK will serve as a source of inspiration to those looking for a new way of life. The techniques which I shall discuss deal with the use of the conscious and subconscious levels of the mind. The use of both will afford a sure means of developing creativeness and favorable personality changes. My book will approach these problems from a psychological point of view. I shall point out clearly a method of achieving success, self-mastery, self-confidence and personal happiness. The techniques are quite simple, yet few people seem to use them. Those who have are well on the road to success, or have already achieved their goals. The simple truths presented in this book are the basis of all success.

I shall show you how easy it is for you to get your subconscious mind to work for what you want. If you are dissatisfied with your present position or station in life, you will be shown how you can change it. You need only use the techniques presented here for a short period of time and you will note the dramatic change in your mental outlook. Life will take on new meaning. Your new found enthusiasm, drive and self-confidence will permeate every phase of your existence. This basic formula for success is not radically new. It is a method that has proven itself over and over again. You will be shown how to harness the power contained in the positive thinking technique. This inspiring book can change your way of life. You have been given an Aladdin's

Lamp. The remarkable power of it is contained within your own mind. You need only be shown how to use it.

I shall give you a blueprint for increasing inner strength. You will be able to achieve for yourself goals that you never dreamed possible. Although this may sound fantastic, it is nevertheless true and you will prove it to yourself. It is never too late to succeed! What others have done, you can do! You yourself need bring to this method only enthusiasm and faith and you will surely reach your pinnacle of success. Here is a golden opportunity. The choice is yours. Your life can be a successful, exciting adventure.

Melvin Powers

12015 Sherman Road
No. Hollywood, California 91605

CHAPTER I

Opportunity Unlimited

THERE IS PERHAPS no greater contradiction to truth nor denunciation of fact than that embodied in the oft-quoted "axiom" which would have us believe that opportunity knocks but once. Were this distressing cliche factual, rather than legendary, it might be well for most of us to subordinate all inspiration, ingenuity and application to the inevitable course of defeat and self-pity. For how many of us have failed to heed that first subtle inkling of opportunity and, subsequently, the knock on the door which proclaimed its arrival. How often has opportunity eluded us, despite our eager determination to herald its first approach, simply because we were not equipped to recognize it as such, and then much later discovered our misconception? How often has opportunity confronted us in the form of a routine incident without the slightest semblance of being a pretentious phenomenon, and then, eventually, through unpredictable circumstances, evolved lamentably, as a mighty potent weapon for accomplishment?

How often, even though we have accurately diagnosed the early symptoms as those belonging to opportunity, have we, after a careful clinical appraisal of their potential resourcefulness, concluded that it would be a matter of good judgment to forfeit this in favor of a future opportunity more suitably attuned to our particular talents or inclinations?

Should all ambition, initiative, and inspiration be condemned to the grim reaper of frustration by one blatant decree of fate which caused us to ignore that first nebulous signal of opportunity? Definitely not!

On the other hand, opportunity will not condone a policy of perpetual rejection. One cannot, through indolence, lack of initiative, doubt, skepticism, fear of innovation, disillusionment, and, above all, negative thinking, reap the benefits of opportunity. The implication is not that opportunity is a jealous, sensitive mistress who will withdraw her favor from an unresponsive suitor, for opportunity is insensitive, indiscriminate, and recurrent. The faculties of the individual for availing himself of the fruits of opportunity will become dull and ineffective with disuse. Though the fertile soil around him become laden with a rich harvest of opportunity, his equipment, dull and rusty, through destructive idleness, will fail to reap the harvest. As does nothing succeed like success, so does nothing fail like failure nurtured from the insidious bosom of negative thought and lack of action.

Do not permit this to happen to you. Be alert to your next big chance for success; be equipped to meet the challenge. I am going to furnish you the necessary tools.

OPPORTUNITY UNLIMITED

Opportunity is always knocking at our door. American markets are constantly receptive to new products. Companies constantly alert to the highly competitive nature of the industrial scene, are eager for new ideas which might enable them to step ahead of the field. Industry is always eager to entertain new ideas, for which millions of dollars are paid each year. New businesses based on a single idea are always starting. These businesses, as a rule, do not require a special skill. They require only an idea. As I write this, I am thinking of the new game, "Scrabble." At this point over one million games have been sold at three dollars apiece followed by the sale of thousands of copies of the book "How To Win At Scrabble." Anyone could have thought of the game. It is a simple idea; just another form of a cross-word puzzle. The game, "Monopoly," too, has sold over a million sets, and here again the idea was simple.

Having the basic idea is not quite all that is necessary. You must sell yourself on the potential of your idea and then formulate your plan to merchandise it. Will you do it overnight? Usually the answer will be no. Many people may try to discourage you. There is latent in human nature a strange quality which repels any suggestion or operation that deviates from the norm. In psychiatric terminology, this is known as neophobia. Generally speaking, people are conservative and addicted to standards of practice which conform to the conventions they have come to regard as standard and workable. By their very existence, these standards are regarded as superior, admitting little by way of modification or improvement. The imagination must be jolted out of its complacency, and enthusiasm must be generated by your own invasive confidence and enthusiasm for what you are attempting to inaugurate.

The important thing to remember is that if you yourself are sold on the merit of your idea you must pursue it to its final conclusion. Submit to your own intuition. Above all, bear in mind this important fact: Apart from matters which require the utmost in technical skill and knowledge, your judgment is as good as the next man's. Believe that it is, know that it is, and take from it the confidence and drive that is so uniquely the byproduct of deep, honest conviction in your own resolutions.

Naturally, you, as a layman, or even a specialist in an unrelated field of endeavor, would not presume to contradict an accredited physician by insisting that what he diagnosed as appendicitis was, in fact, a hyper-acidity of the stomach, merely because you entertained a certain enthusiasm for hyper-acidity.

It is not only experience, but years of highly skilled training and academic knowledge that you are seeking to contravert here. However, eliminate the skilled training and the academics. Reduce the situation to one wherein you are pitting your judgment only against the matter of experience, and you should be far less reticent about venturing an opinion on the subject. To refute the advantages of experience would be more than a little ridiculous. To submit as inviolate the theory that experience precludes the validity of contradictory opinion predicated on lack of experience, would be equally ridiculous. Do not allow yourself to become discouraged merely because you feel the person discounting your views is fortified with more experience than you possess. Respect it, of course. But do not become awed by it to the extent that it stifles your own imagination and opinions. If, after making proper allowance for the other's advantage of experience, you are still favorably inclined toward your own opinion, by all means place full reliance on your own judgment. Should you ultimately find that you are wrong, your decision will at least have been the mistake of your own honest judgment. There is enormously more consolation in this than in the realization that your error was the result of faith in the miscalculated judgment of another.

In support of the premise that experience is not an irrefutable advantage, and should not be permitted to restrict independence of thought and deed, you need only to look in any direction around you to find situations wherein aggressive, positive thinking men capable of sound judgment and decision have forged ahead of men of considerably more experience, who have become smugly complacent in the assumed invulnerability of their greater experience.

Too often does the assurance that stems from long experience fail to yield to modification required by changing conditions and circumstances, and in these instances its effectiveness is considerably reduced sometimes to a degree that would render it less valuable than none at all.

So bear in mind the importance of independent thought, and reliance on independent judgment. Do not be discouraged by contradictory opinions based upon greater experience. Your thought might have been predicated on new facts, fresh circumstances and altered conditions which the other man did not take into account. There is a danger latent in all experience: the failure to constantly subject your store of knowledge to the test of change continually going on in our realm of existence.

To illustrate, let us resort to a broad and ludicrous example, but one which, nevertheless, demonstrates the point. Assume that you are a physician, Doctor X, fresh out of school, equipped with all the knowledge that your textbooks, laboratories, and instructors have been able to furnish, but, naturally, sadly lacking in one essential —experience. Dr. Y is a reputable physician, of many, many years of experience, and has become lulled into the state of security that often accompanies the know-how attending experience. Dr. Y examines the stricken patient and correctly diagnoses the illness as being pneumonia. Whereupon, he reaches down into his fund of experience and comes up with a suggested remedy. The patient fails to respond and death appears imminent. You, Dr. X, are called in, and upon examination, also diagnose the illness as pneumonia. You are told what remedies Dr. Y has administered. You have considerable respect for the great experience that you know to be Dr. Y's stock in trade. If you are awed by his experience to a degree which stifles your own independent thought and imagination, you will yield to his greater experience, abandon your own ideas, and allow the patient to die. If you are not to be overcome by the magnitude of his experience, you will rely on your own independently calculated opinion which suggested that in this particular case, a new drug will help, and the patient survives. Dr. Y has become overly complacent in, and reliant upon, his experience, without subjecting it to the constant test of innovation and new circumstances. Therefore, he was not aware of the new magic drug. You lack his experience, but your opinon was based upon fresh independent thought which refused to be thwarted by a contradictory conclusion predicated upon greater experience. And yours is the glorious satisfaction that comes from formulating your own judgment, and acting according.

If I have cloaked this point with a seeming redundancy, it was for the express purpose of conveying to you the importance of independent thought and reliance upon your own judgment. If you are convinced of that, you are already equipped with one of the most potent and resourceful implements in our tool chest of success.

In every era of prosperity there is talk of economic recession to follow. The years immediately following war years are generally plush in the economic by-product of industrial recovery. There is a frantic drive to resuscitate inventories depleted by the necessity of having diverted all resources to the war effort. Employment attains new peaks; new commodities are bought up as soon as they reach the sales floors; price ceases to become an issue and prosperity permeates the entire economic system. Eventually, there comes the leveling off period when the laws of economics again take over. The boom that existed during and immediately after the war years is at an end. But should this mean that opportunity is lost? Of course not.

We hear talk now of a recession. It is true that business in general is not as booming as it was during the war years. But should this mean that opportunity is lost? Of course not. I would venture to say that opportunity is greater than ever, because getting back to a normal period of competition requires greater ingenuity and resourcefulness from all branches of business.

You may ask, "Where do I fit into this picture of commerce? How can I do something creative when I don't have the opportunity?" There are answers. Do you work for an employer? Then try to find a better and more efficient way of doing things at your own job. If you come up with an idea to improve or expedite your portion of the work tell it to your employer. He will be grateful to you. The important thing is to get the thinking wheels in motion in your own mind. We want to dust off the cobwebs, so to speak, and start you thinking in a constructive manner. If you are self-employed, you can try to think of better ways of doing your work, or of ways to stimulate your sales or improve your services. Chances are that you are not working at top efficiency. Why not set aside ten minutes every day, either in the morning or just before retiring, to this task of constructive thinking. Ideas will come to you. There is a specialized technique to be used, which we will discuss thoroughly later in the book.

Are you discouraged with things in general? Do you feel that opportunity will never visit you? You are wrong! Discouragement is the very thing that you must fight. How do you do it? You do it by forcing yourself to change your mental attitude. Don't dwell on your failures. Instead think of your success.

Necessity many times is the springboard for success. Many a poor boy has become a millionaire because his early poverty impelled him to achievement. Often such a person was not an especially good talker, and many times he did not have the advantage of higher education. Yet, to the surprise of many he achieved a high station in life. What was the asset that somehow forged him and others like him ahead? It was determination, faith in his own ability, and enthusiasm for what he was doing.

The president of the Necchi Sewing Machine Company was a refugee from Poland. When he came to the United States several years ago he was penniless. His only trade was fixing sewing machines, but he had a burning desire to achieve success. He was the first to import the Necchi sewing machine from Italy. Within a relatively short period of time he built a million dollar concern.

Look at the successful people in your own community. Have they all had college educations? Were their positions just handed to them? Did they all inherit their wealth? Did success just happen to come their way? You will find they have one common denominator, and that is, all of them possessed a vital enthusiasm for their work. They were consistent in the furtherance of their goals, and they believed in their own abilities.

You may say that the same opportunities that existed years ago do not exist today. That is true. Today's opportunities are different, but greater in number. If your idea has merit you can capitalize on it almost overnight. Years ago we did not have the mass distribution systems and the mass communication that we have today. Think of all the products that are sold through magazines and newspapers. Radio and television offer other vast media for reaching the public. Many products owe their quick success to television. I am sure that many of you have seen the advertising for Charles Antell Formula No. 9 on your television sets. I, myself, started using this hair preparation after I had seen it very cleverly advertised on television.

Just think of how many ball point pens have been sold in recent years because of effective advertising. Yet the ball point pen was not a radically new idea. It was merely an improvement on an existent article; an improvement that made pens "leak proof." I don't have to tell you the results. You yourself probably own several ball point pens.

The book-publishing industry has been able to increase its sales by millions of books each year because someone had the foresight to print popular books in pocket editions to sell at twenty-five cents apiece in addition to the larger and heavier bound versions which sell for three and four dollars a copy. Normally the average book sells about five thousand copies. Now the initial run on any pocket size book is two hundred and fifty thousand copies, and many have sold over the million mark. This idea could have occurred to anyone. The idea of a comic book started a billion dollar industry.

I have pointed out these few examples to show you that opportunities are always there for those who are willing to put on their thinking caps and devote a little time toward reaching their goals. Ideas will come to you automatically, once you begin to channelize your thinking. Don't submit to the course of least resistance, which would have you believe that there is nothing new under the sun; that there is no idea which might occur to you which hasn't already occurred to someone else; that if the idea were of any value, surely it would have been thought of by someone before. This could be amazingly far from the truth. Obviously, were this attitude the rule rather than the exception, new ideas would never be unearthed; we would soon become a stagnant, decadent society. Your idea may be fresh, unique, imaginative. If you feel it has merit, don't treat it lightly; above all, don't reject it. Give it the acid test by putting it to work. If it fails, you will at least enjoy the satisfaction of having tried. If it succeeds, you will enjoy the profound gratification of having made a distinct contribution to the social order. One successful idea will inspire others. They may not all be good, but eventually you will come up with several that will be rewarding, and you may be sure, no reward you will ever receive will be half as satisfying as that which resulted from a creation of your own ingenuity.

The ideas that came from suggestion boxes during the war did much to accelerate the war effort. Most of these ideas came from individuals who ordinarily would never have thought of improving any particular system or product. The most amazing thing about it was that in many cases people without technical training were able to suggest improvements for highly complicated machinery, the reason being that they applied their personal experiences to the particular problem involved. They were able to see the problem in a light radically different from that of the highly trained technician. The incentive of helping the war effort, plus a monetary reward, compelled many people to think along creative lines for the first time. A surprising number of the ideas were good, and all major companies still use the suggestion box, not only for suggestions concerning their products and methods of production, but also for suggestions on how to improve labor-management relations.

You may say at this point, "All this sounds fine but how can I get started in a concrete way?" You may be blaming others for your lack of progress. You may be blaming your family for not encouraging you, or for giving you inadequate education, or for limiting your opportunities for success. Your complaint may be valid, but if you continue to carry on as you have in the past and carry a chip on your shoulder, the next ten years will find you exactly where you are today. You may well be your own liability. Why not become an asset to yourself by making up your mind that from this time forth you will seek only the constructive forces in life; the forces that spell success! It is my feeling that one usually causes his own failure and defeat. Remember that others in worse circumstances than yours have overcome all obstacles and achieved what they desired in life. This is the point to keep in mind. Success comes many times as the result of setbacks, and the strong desire to overcome them.

Herbert Hoover was orphaned at the age of seven. He missed the warmth and love of parents and the guidance that is so important in the planning of a career, and yet he grew up to become President of the United States. His could not have been an easy task. What impelled this achievement? The answer must be found in his mental attitude.

The late Franklin Delano Roosevelt led the country out of a severe depression and on the road to victory in World War II, in spite of the physical handicap resulting from infantile paralysis. Four times he was elected to the presidency of our country, and his name lives now in the hearts of all free men. His life is a symbol to all who desire success despite problems that press them. I could go on citing examples, but the point is apparent. You will succeed if you fervently believe that you can.

Creativeness is the backbone of America. What would life be like today without the creative imaginations of men like the Wright Brothers, Eastman, Edison, Marconi, Ford, and the many others who contributed so greatly to the welfare of all peoples? None of these men were immediate successes. They had their problems, their trials, their setbacks. People looked upon them as being weird and impractical. What would most people have said to you fifteen years ago if you had declared that soon almost everyone in the large cities of America would have a television set in his own home? Men with ideas must be ready to encounter discouragement and sometimes ridicule. But their drive, initiative, and confidence will make them the winners, the pace setters, the doers of our time.

We have the highest standard of living in the world today. We have the techniques and facilities for the greatest production that the world has ever seen. There is now, and always will be, room for your idea, your product, or your system or service. You needn't be an expert in the production or distribution end of your product. You need only the idea.

You may say, "I have a wonderful idea, but I don't have the money to put it over." Don't worry about it. There are any number of individuals who are eager to invest in a good idea. Your local bank might be interested in your proposition. We all know that fortunes have been made from single ideas. If you are sincerely sold on your idea, impart it to someone who has the means of seeing it pushed to a successful conclusion.

However, before you tie yourself up financially, seek the guidance of an attorney. He will be able to help you protect your interest and your idea, and to see that you obtain proper compensation for them.

CHAPTER II

It Is Never Too Late to Find Success

YOU MAY BE THINKING that all of this talk about positive thinking sounds fine, but that somehow it doesn't apply to you. I am aware that you have probably been at your present job for quite some time; that possibly you know only one type of work; that you have responsibilities; that you are just tied down. I only ask that for two weeks you apply what you learn from reading this book. If it doesn't start you in the right direction drop me a personal note. Perhaps I can offer you some suggestions that would apply to your special case. For those of you who are just starting on your careers, this material should serve as an invaluable adjunct in helping you to find your mark in life.

There are thousands of authenticated case histories of poor boys who became wealthy, of persons who started their search for careers quite late in life, and succeeded. Don't you often read of individuals who are grandparents going to college? They are finally fulfilling an impelling desire that they have always had. Evening schools are enrolled to capacity. Everyone is seeking self-improvement. Never think that it is too late for you, in spite of your circumstances. You will find that life can still not only be more rewarding for you, but also richer, fuller, and more satisfying.

It is never necessary to resign yourself to haphazard living. There is always new meaning to be found in ordinary activity. I am reminded of the radio program, "Life Can Be Beautiful." Does this sound trite? I would say that it does not. I would rather be the optimist than the pessimist. We all know that a person can talk himself into becoming physically and mentally ill. Do not be one of those individuals who talks himself into remaining at a status-quo position all through life. You may be on that road already. Make up your mind this very moment to forge ahead. Do it to the surprise and amazement of your family and friends. They will be rooting for you.

We are not living in a hostile world. You can find many examples of good will towards one's neighbor. Your own attitude will determine how people will react to you.

Start now to develop optimism. Cultivate the idea that you are not limited, regardless of circumstances. You probably have abilities of which you are not even aware. Do not accept the idea that you are only fit for one type of job. You have probably heard of people, paralyzed and confined to bed for many years, managing to get up and walk when threatened by some immediate danger. They are galvanized into action by an urgent need. So can you be jolted out of your lethargy and self pity by the ideas in this book.

A person may make himself an invalid after hearing that he has a heart condition. He may confine himself to bed and limit his acitivity to waiting for the worst to happen. On the other hand, he can adopt the attitude of slowing down a bit and still get the most out of life. Which one of these individuals have you been? Remember, it is never too late to take a positive step. We can do wonders with our minds if only we adhere to optimism and faith.

Do the best that you can in any given task. That is all that is ever required of you. The future has a way of taking care of itself. One's station in life reflects one's thinking. We know that the converse of this is true as well; that is, one's thinking reflects one's station in life. Let us take advantage of the wisdom of this statement and start to use the power of positive thinking in everything that we do. One cannot find success haphazardly. One must devote time and thought and energy to it, and then it will surely come. The inner power that is dormant in our minds can be aroused and directed by holding only propitious thoughts. Creativeness stems from the subconscious mind. Our aim is to get a positive subconscious and then to link our conscious with it. The sole object of this book is to get you to alter your mental attitude and channelize your thinking towards self-improvement. We must emphasize again that it is never too late, no matter what the circumstances. We all have the faculty for enjoying a well rounded life. The road to achievement is not always easy, of course, but we can help to ease the burden by proper direction and the utilization of those factors that have helped countless others. Let us learn by example.

Which of us has not experienced disappointment? Perhaps it is all in the pattern of life. Actually nobody can prevent us from achieving success, once we put doubt and fear out of our minds.

We do not discard an old piano or violin because it is out of tune. We proceed to tune it. I should like to draw an analogy between one's mental faculties and the sound components of a piano. If one or two or more notes of a piano are out of tune the piano is not worthless. It can still be used satisfactorily provided we do not strike these notes. If we do strike these notes we immediately hear discord. We could continue playing with this discord but, instead, we do the obvious thing and tune the string so that it will harmonize with the other notes. If we do not do this, obviously we will get the same discord every time we strike the ailing keys.

In dealing with personality structure are we not likened to the piano? Usually where there is a minor psychological problem there is a discord in some phases of the personality. But the entire personality has not disintegrated. As long as the individual with the problem is not confronted with the type of stimuli which will cause his personal discord he can function adequately. But the possibility of discord is always there. To function properly and efficiently he should try to correct whatever maladjustment he may have.

If a piano string does not respond properly, we proceed to tighten the peg that holds it until the proper tone is reached. This is simple enough to do. Usually nothing is actually wrong with the string itself. The anchor has merely become a little loose, and a slight adjustment will bring the string back into harmony with the other keys.

Can we deal with the personality in a similar manner? I think we can. For example, where there is a lack of confidence we know that the person is not responding properly to a stimulus or stimuli. How can we get this person in tune? We need to reach the subconscious mind to make the adjustment, for here lies the response mechanism of the personality. These responses are usually of an involuntary nature. Have you ever heard a person say, "I wish I weren't this way, but I can't seem to do anything about it." He is actually saying, "I have been conditioned somehow to respond unfavorably in spite of myself, and I cannot seem to overcome this conditioned response." Our tuning implements consist of words and thoughts; thoughts made up of words. Words have meaning. The interpretation of words may be different at times, but basically we all respond in a similar manner. If I say, "Think of your favorite food," you can all visualize the food and perhaps even attain a strong desire for it. The key, then, is to instill firmly in the mind those positive thoughts which will elicit positive, desirable responses.

If we do this consistently, we shall gradually come "in tune." Our personalities will respond in the manner which we truly desire, and feelings, of inseurity, anxiety, tension and fear will be replaced with feelings of self-confidence. It is like the tuning of the piano string. We respond to a given situation in accordance with the previous training of our subconscious. If this previous tuning has been wrong, we must re-tune. The expression of a subconscious that has been filled with positive suggestions can only be that of enthusiasm, hope, determination, confidence and self-reliance. Begin now to implant these positive affirmations. Lift your chin high; begin the task, and you will succeed.

Some will say that the reason that they are not successful at an age where they think they should be is because they were not given any encouragement as children. They will say that they never had any real parental guidance in choosing a life work, or never had the opportunity of seeking guidance from a vocational counselor. It is true that children who are fortunate enough to be so guided fit themselves much more easily into adult careers. But there is no reason to despair over the early lack of such help. It is never too late to acquire good vocational guidance. All large colleges and many social organizations maintain staffs of competent vocational counselors. For a very reasonable fee, and sometimes without charge of any kind, they will give you a series of tests that will determine your aptitudes, talents and abilities. There is no age limit for taking these tests, which, by the way, have been made up by the leading psychologists and foremost educators of our country. These tests are well worth looking into, especially for those of you who are not sure of exactly what you would like to be doing.

IT IS NEVER TOO LATE TO FIND SUCCESS

In addition to guidance, there are two other important factors in the picture of success. One is confidence. A man must believe that he can be successful in his chosen profession. Nobody is born with confidence. It is acquired through environment. It is never too early to start suggesting to a child that he has confidence. The other important factor is love. Success in any endeavor is not rewarding in itself unless that success can be shared with someone. That someone can be a parent, wife, friend or anyone dear to you. The desire to share is motivated by love. One of the strongest reasons for striving for success is the knowledge that this loved one will find pleasure and satisfaction in it. A man will work more diligently when he knows his family will share in the rewards of his labor. If one does not have the impetus of love, one lacks the spark that makes climbing the ladder of success that much easier.

I believe that another contributing factor toward success is a sound philosophy of life. Everyone has some philosophy, of course. It is reflected in everything that he does. But this philosophy must extend outward to include others and not be selfishly self-centered if it would succeed. We should affiliate ourselves with causes that work toward the betterment of mankind. We must be interested in the welfare of others as well as our own. Cast your bread upon the waters and the rewards will be great. Have you ever given any thought to the wealthy people who contribute to charities? It would seem that they are always giving to worthy causes, and yet they never run out of money. This is something to think about. These people do not hold onto every dollar. They share their riches with others. Some of the most successful business men I know are leaders in charitable work. If you fail to share, you lose out on one of the greatest joys of living.

You, the reader, may say, "All this philosophy sounds fine but do you really believe that I can find success at my age?" My answer is an unequivocal YES! You have the experience of living, experience in your work, experience in personal relationships with people. You may say, looking back over lost opportunities, "If I only knew then what I know now, things would certainly be different." But is it really too late for achievement? Evidently you do not really feel this to be true or you would not be reading this book. You must possess hope, determination and faith. These, my friend, are really all that are necessary at this point. Now start to use your imagination. All business enterprises, inventions and products began in someone's imagination. Let it begin in yours.

Cultivate your imagination. Use it for your success. Put aside ten minutes every day for thinking. Relax in a quiet place and give yourself up to thought. Visualize what you can do to improve some product in which you are interested, or try to conjure up a new product. See if you can develop a service or improve upon an existing service. You have heard of shopping services, phone exchange services, diaper services, and a hundred other types. Just look in the yellow pages of your telephone book. Perhaps you can bring to your community a needed service, or think of a new one. Usually you need very little capital to begin. If the idea has merit, it will pay for itself. Proceed diligently along these lines and ideas will come to you just as surely as you are reading this book.

If, on the other hand, you "cry the blues" about your situation and want sympathy, then, of course, nothing will take place. I ask again, "Who has led the ideal life?" Certainly very few. We must be strong and look toward the future. Ignore what has happened in your past. Gain by your experience, and create a new future for yourself.

Let me tell you the story of a friend. This young man volunteered for service in the United States Army at the beginning of World War II. He served with valor in New Guinea and in the Philippines, and was decorated for bravery. When the war had been won he returned to New York City to resume his work as a machinist. There he met the girl who is now his wife. They decided to begin their life together in California; they felt this would be best for their future and health. He obtained employment easily for he was an excellent machinist. As he began to save a little money, his wife spoke to him about opening his own machine shop. She felt that he had the ability and know-how to do it. But my friend did not agree. He felt secure in his job, and didn't believe himself capable of self-employment. They confided to me that his life with his parents had not been ideal. These parents had always told him that he would never amount to much; that he was a good machinist, but did not have a business head. This had made a very deep impression in his mind. He continued to believe their words true.

To make a long story short, my friend finally did go into business for himself, after the repeated urging of his wife. Within two years he grossed a quarter of a million dollars. Today, four short years later, he employs fifty people and is the picture of a confident individual.

This preceding story shows that one need not remain in a particular position for life. One can advance, if only he has the determination to do so. An interesting part of the story is that the words of his parents had left such a deep impression upon his mind that he probably would never have achieved his success, had it not been for an encouraging and understanding wife. She did not dwell on the shortcomings of her husband, nor did she condemn his parents. Instead she pointed out his proficiency as a machinist which helped fire his imagination. That dream, that picture of a prosperous machine shop has become a reality for them. At the beginning of his business venture when the going was rough this wife remained by her husband's side, helping to do the bookkeeping and encouraging him with her love and belief. My friend told me that when the going was difficult he did not give up, because he wanted to make good for her. He wanted her to be proud of him. I can predict a very bright future for this couple.

Is it too late for you? No, it is never too late to find success. Take personal inventory of yourself. You will be surprised to find the assets that you possess. Never mind your shortcomings. No one is perfect. Have you heard Johnny Mercer's song "Accentuate the Positive?" Take its advice. Dwell on your assets and incorporate them for your success.

Chapter III

The Importance of Positive Thinking

I AM SURE THAT every one of my readers has heard something within the last few years about the importance of positive thinking. Numerous books have been written on this subject, and countless lectures concerning it have been given. The important question is, "What have you done about directing your thoughts along these lines?"

If you agree there is something in this science of positive thought, but never use it for yourself, then you are not employing your best judgment. I have had countless people tell me about a wonderful inspirational book that they have read, or a wonderful sermon or lecture they have heard, and they will go on expounding the subject matter with great enthusiasm. When I ask them if they have put into practice any of the material gained, they usually reply in the negative, or give me some excuse as to why they haven't done so. Here is a very important point that I wish to bring to my readers. If you agree with the contents of this book and fail to apply it, then certainly you have wasted your time and energy in reading the book. I urge you to start looking at the bright side of things. Start thinking in a positive manner.

One must learn to control his mental attitude. This requires self-discipline and a constancy of purpose. I am sure that you have heard someone say "It is his own thinking that keeps him down." Of course this is true. We must fill our minds with positive thoughts at all times.

We must saturate our minds with the idea of success, and success will finally come to us. Our associations as well as our environment should reflect this type of thinking. No one ever became a success in life by spending his time at the local beer parlor. There are too many people "crying in their beer" so to speak. If you listen to them long enough, you will find yourself trapped by them and their negative ideas.

One is a product of one's thinking. You have achieved your present goal because you knew you could handle it. Now the task is to set a higher goal for yourself. You might say "I have been at my job too long. I can't change now." But this is the talk of a pessimist. The important thing is to sincerely believe in yourself. Start this new train of thinking.

Take inventory of yourself each day, and decide whether the day has afforded anything unusual which might amplify your stock of resourceful experiences. Did you contribute something to your own personal advancement, or did you merely fulfill the routine duties and details required of you in your employment? Regardless of how meager and seemingly insignificant, do something each day which will, in some measure, add to the

ultimate fulfillment of your goal in life. These
of accomplishment will add up, and eventually
themselves on your tally sheet of achievement. A day in
which you have done nothing to further your determined
purpose in life is a worthless day, regardless of your
earnings for the discharge of your routine duties. On
the other hand, a day in which you are honestly convinced that you have aided the course of realizing your
goal, is a day which has brought you inestimable for-
tune. Obviously, this is relevant only to the man who
has set a goal for himself. It is difficult to stress—certainly impossible to over-emphasize—the prime importance of a goal as a necessary ingredient to success.
Actually, without a goal there can be no success in the
true sense of the word, for how can you ever know that
you have achieved it? I would not presume to set up one
circumstance and tell you that only when you have accomplished it have you achieved success, for the determination of what constitutes success must, in the final
analysis, rest with you. People think differently about
success. To one person it may represent the accumulation of money, to another, power, to another, good
health, to another, a compatible marriage, to another,
a good reputation, and so forth into the limitless facets
of accomplishment. I shall, however, with unalterable
conviction tell you that regardless of what it may be,
you have achieved success when you have attained the
goal you set for yourself.

It therefore becomes apparent that you must establish a goal in life, and your every effort should be direc-

ted toward its ultimate and inevitable fulfillment. True, many people ramble through life and eventually stumble into a circumstance which they interpret
as success, and at that point decide that this was their
goal, but this is definitely a converse approach to
achievement. It contains none of the challenge, the incentive, the inspiration, that results from setting up a
target of accomplishment, and pays off none of the
eventual gratification of scoring that vitally important
bull's eye of success. Above all, set no false goals for
yourself. To be a true goal, it must be one which you
honestly want; one in which you believe, one to which
above all else in life you are willing to delegate all effort, ingenuity and application, without compromise. If
your goal meets these requirements, it will be charged
with incentive and inspiration, and you will eventually
discover that automatically your efforts will incline toward the attainment of your goal. But let me reiterate,
this will only become possible when the goal you have
set up is a true goal—one you have chosen as something you want above all else out of life. Too often
people allow others to establish their goals for them, and
the results are generally disastrous. Parents, naturally
ambitious for the welfare of their child, will prema-
turely select for him a trade or profession, simply because it gratifies their own sense of accomplishment;
well-meaning friends, often lamenting their own dismal
predicaments, will seek to steer the subject toward a
goal which they themselves regret not having chosen.
The subject himself might settle on a goal simply be-

cause it represents to him some person for whom he entertains a profound respect or admiration.

Remember, what you have chosen as your goal is not nearly as important as that you really want to achieve it. If it is something you really want and something in which you really believe, you will derive from it all the inspiration, drive and enthusiasm necessary to eventually accomplish it.

What are some of the personal attributes or desirable traits of personality that help to promote success? I shall enumerate a few.

First of all, you must be optimistic at all times. Yes, even though things look gloomy, be an optimist. Look at the positive side of things. Perhaps some of you have heard this example of the difference between an optimist and a pessimist. The pessimist says that the glass of water is half empty while the optimist says that the glass of water is half full. Try to keep your mind from dwelling upon the negative aspects of things.

Remember the biblical story of David and Goliath. David slew the giant Goliath and won freedom for his people. Goliath, himself, laughed at David, but David was determined. He had a purpose, a goal to fulfill, and he believed in his power to fulfill it. Yes, David was an optimist and his optimism saved the day.

If you maintain a negative attitude, you will never achieve what you desire. A positive, dynamic attitude is contagious. We all face seemingly insurmountable obstacles, and yet with the proper attitude and desire nothing is really insurmountable.

I am sure that you have heard of miracle cures. People with various types of mental and physical ailments travel to shrines, where they have heard others have been cured. They drink the holy water or pray in the holy shrine, according to the accepted ritual, and many of them receive instantaneous cures. Their faith laid the ground work, so to speak, and what they firmly believed would happen did happen. You are what you think you are. If you think failure, then you inevitably fail. The reverse is equally true. Think only of success and you cannot possibly avoid it.

Over the years I have made a careful analysis of the thinking of those who have been successful in their chosen field. I have also been interested in the type of lives they have lived. I can tell you that the secret of their success is constancy of purpose. Does this sound too simple? Even if it does, it is true, and we certainly can all do something about it. A man with determination will always succeed. Most of the successful men to whom I have spoken did not place too much stress on the importance of education or technical training. Of course, they realized its value, but they felt that the true purpose of education was to develop sound reasoning ability. They felt that the same result could be achieved through actual experience on a job as through formal schooling. In other words, you need not feel that you are limited because of lack of education.

THE IMPORTANCE OF POSITIVE THINKING

It is true that one of the principal contributions of education to success, is an adroit regimentation of the thinking process. But lack of education assuredly does not preclude you from developing this facility. Positive thinking, if assiduously practiced, will tend to effect a strict regimentation of thought in the direction of your goal.

I feel that the important thing to aim for in helping yourself is a change in attitude. We have spoken about the importance of positive thinking. In addition we need such personality traits as earnestness, fairmindedness, and determination. You can derive great benefits from adopting these attributes along with your positive thinking. I have seen the combination work countless times, and I can assure you that it will work for you. It takes a little practice on your part but it is a wonderful pastime. What could be better than doing something for your self-improvement? It is not a selfish goal, for many will benefit by it—your family, friends, and community. But you have to be your own cheer leader.

In speaking to various sales managers, I have found that a common complaint has been that the salesmen lose enthusiasm for their work after they have been on the job for a time. My objective in addressing sales groups is to generate new feelings of enthusiasm. If I have done this, then I have been successful, and the up swing on the sales chart will indicate this re-charging of enthusiasm.

Positive thinking without action or enthusiasm is of little, if any, value. I have heard people say, "I used this idea of positive thinking and it didn't do anything for me." Can we account for that? I believe that we can. A lot of people have the "prove it to me" attitude. It would seem they were belligerent to the very idea of positive thinking. I can assure you that it will be difficult for them to achieve success from any mode of philosophy, treatment, or therapy. What these people are actually afraid of is to open their minds to anything new. They distrust innovation. These are the people that impede the progress of any undertaking. However, they can be dealt with by re-education, by the process of reasoning, and by example.

Have you ever given any thought to the reason why one place of business, selling the same products as its nearby competitor, shows a good profit while the other just manages to squeeze by, or is on the verge of failure? Haven't you been approached by several persons rendering the same service and shown preference for one? Why was this so? Let us say, for example, that it was a certain type of insurance. Both representatives were selling the exact same coverage. The price was exactly the same. Why did you pick one over the other? The decisive element is always personal. One salesman reflected more confidence than the other. His confidence stemmed from positive thinking.

What can you gain by this little example? I see it this way. It doesn't matter what you are selling or what service you are rendering. Actually, you are selling yourself ninety percent of the time.

I am thinking of an outstanding lingerie salesman whom I know. He is a man who has only a grammar school education. His family was extremely poor, and he sold newspapers to help supplement the family income. He was glad to do his share and did not bemoan the fact that it was necessary for him to help out while his playmates were going to school.

You might think that this young man would grow up with a chip on his shoulder. He did not, for he was brought up in a house filled with love and tenderness. When he spoke to his parents of his aspirations, he was given encouragement. They lent him the moral support that is so necessary for success. This man today makes about $50,000 a year in commissions as the leading New England representative of various lingerie concerns in the country. Manufacturers are always after him to handle their lines.

I was privileged to accompany this master salesman on several of his calls. What was his approach? What was his secret? He greeted everyone with a warm, sincere, friendly smile. This genuine friendliness was contagious. He was interested in people. He was interested in the success that the buyer was having with her past purchases. He did not press for a sale. He gave an honest appraisal of what was selling well at the time and suggested what he thought best for the buyer. This technique worked wonders for him. He was always welcome.

I questioned him as to his formula for success. He told me, "Always keep a cheerful disposition no matter how tough the sledding." The success that he now enjoys was not easily gained. But he practices his philosophy, and has been enjoying the fruits of his positive thinking for many years.

His brother is one of the most prominent attorneys in Boston. He studied law at night, while keeping a day time job. This was not an easy task but he persevered and passed the bar examination with flying colors. This distinguished attorney, who is extremely wealthy now, used positive thinking, but his method was not identical with that of his brother. He was more religiously inclined and he told me that he derived, and still does derive, a great deal of his strength from prayer. When he felt like giving up his studies for the bar examination and, later, when he found it extremely difficult to make a living as a young attorney, he turned to prayer and, somehow, was given renewed strength and hope.

I would like to tell you of a little incident that shows the thinking of this attorney. I was visiting at his home one evening, and while we were sitting in his den, I noticed that he was putting crisp five dollar bills in various envelopes. I was interested because I noticed that these envelopes were going to different charities throughout the world. It seemed to me that there were about sixty of these envelopes. I asked about this and he told me, "You get out of life, only what you give to it."

THE IMPORTANCE OF POSITIVE THINKING

Both brothers have found true success in life. Both have achieved success by holding firmly to the psychology of positive thinking. Both brothers lead rich spiritual lives as well, one more than the other, but who can measure individual needs? If you are religiously inclined, use the power of prayer. It is one of the most stirring and energizing forces for good in the world. If you haven't been to a religious service in a long time, why don't you attend one this week? It will do you good. It will give you a needed lift and inspiration. Please note that I am not suggesting religion as the key to solving all your problems, but I am suggesting that we should all try to lead more spiritual lives.

As I re-read what I have just written, I cannot help but think of the great humanitarian and leader, Abraham Lincoln. Surely, everyone knows something of his biography. Most people are familiar with the struggles of this great man, who studied by firelight after toiling strenuously all day long. Here again is a familiar example of a person who was determined to overcome all odds. He was defeated many times for public office, but he continued to seek it. He carried the philosophy of positive thinking all through his life.

You may have read how he walked many miles in the rain to return the change to a widow who had purchased some articles in his store, and had forgotten to take the money. Here was a man with feeling for his fellow human beings. He was not selfish in his determination to succeed. This poor farm boy, without formal educa-

tion, who became one of the great presidents and personalities of all times, was aptly nicknamed Honest Abe.

I am sure that you have read the story of Abraham
Lincoln and the many hardships that he overcame before
he was elected to the presidency. History unfolds countless stories of how great men have won out over seemingly insurmountable difficulties. Like them, you need
only harness your potential energy, and success will be
yours.

I could give you numerous other examples, but I feel
that those above will suffice. Do they give you inspiration? I certainly hope they do. I am sure that you know
people among your own associates who have become
successful "the hard way" so to speak. There is an Italian
proverb that reads "Non c'e beneficio senza sacrificio."
The translation of this is, "There is no benefit without
a sacrifice." How wise and true this is. If we want the
good things in life, we must work for them. If you are
willing to work diligently toward your goal, you will
surely succeed. Remember the importance of positive
thinking at all times. It will help you attain success in
spite of any obstacles which may be in your way.

CHAPTER IV

The Magic of
Painting Mental Pictures

YES, THERE IS MAGIC in painting mental pictures. Some people call this day-dreaming. If the mind can conceive of an idea, then the idea can become a reality. If you can visualize yourself in some desirable situation, then it can be brought about. The people who achieve success in life are usually dreamers, in the sense that they are able to paint mental pictures of the future, and the role that they will play in it. Of course, one must have his two feet on the ground as well, but the use of the technique of painting mental pictures will give you the impetus that may be needed to start you on your road to success.

One's attitude determines his future. It is never too late to change the future. We need only the desire to change and the desire to forge ahead, and then if we proceed in a logical manner, we will succeed.

I have said that the use of the imagination in painting mental pictures is one of the important techniques in achieving your goal. Try this technique. Picture yourself as being already possessed of those things that you truly desire. Visualize them as being yours now. If you do it successfully, you will note an immediate change in your personality. It will be an automatic change. Let me give you an example of this. Picture yourself a millionaire possessed of a beautiful mansion and all that goes with millions. Just close your eyes and visualize this for one minute. Do it now.

Put down this book for a minute, after which you can continue with your reading. Did you note something happening to you? Did you feel a change in your personality? If your picturing was sufficiently vivid you would have noted the change. You see how our attitudes can change our future. We need only keep a desired image in our mind and sooner or later we will become the reflection of this image.

Dreams can serve as a constant reminder of that which we seek to achieve. They are the inexhaustible fountains of inspiration that impel us toward an achievement of what they represent. Dreams, for the most part, except those which on occasion invade our subconscious mind during sleep, are nothing more than imaginary manifestations of that which we seek to eventually translate into actual experience. The power of dreams to inspire and activate the facilities of accomplishment is an actual and potent factor in the success pattern.

Does this sound as though you must be a dreamer? Yes, I would say in a sense one must be a dreamer, but remember that all success in life is based upon dreams. Only the dreamers conceive new goals and reach them despite the obstacles in their way.

It doesn't matter whether you are aiming for a better life, a better career, or a new invention. The technique is the same. Our great nation was once a dream in the minds of men who sought freedom of thought and religion. From this dream the entire world has profited. This pattern is the same in all realms of progress. Dream, visualize, then reproduce the dream in concrete form. It is important for us to follow this pattern of progress to achieve our own success.

The United Nations was at one time a dream and a prayer in the hearts of men, a dream of securing world peace for all people. This world governing-body has become a reality in spite of the cynicism and the hindrances of organized pressure groups made up of those opposed to change. All progress must contend with the narrowmindedness of these recurrent groups.

If you are so unfortunate as to discuss your idea with one of these individuals, I needn't tell you the result. You will come away a discouraged person. It is always so easy to criticize. We all tend to do it. Why not use the same energy for constructive tackling of the problem. Don't be an arm chair general! I am sure that you know people who are always saying "Something should be done about this situation." This is the extent of their contribution. They never tackle the problem itself. Don't you fall into this type of thinking; it will hinder your progress in all fields. Visualize the successful solution to the problem and proceed in a logical manner to work it out.

A prominent attorney once sought my help to rid himself of a dreadful fear of speaking before a jury. He had usually given his trial work to one of his associates in his office because of this uncontrollable fear. I suggested that he use the technique of painting mental pictures to help him overcome his problem. Here is the technique! I suggested that he lie down, close his eyes, and visualize himself talking to the jury. He reported that he felt then the same panic that he had felt whenever he had actually spoken to the jury. He told me he could feel his heart beating faster. His hands were perspiring. I told him to continue with his mental image. As the tension subsided, I told him to imagine himself next as a confident, well-poised attorney.

He did and gradually a new feeling of self-assuredness began to take hold. By using this technique for several weeks, he was finally able to try a case. Yes, he did experience a recurrence of the fear this time again, but it gradually vanished by this relatively simple process. He had instilled a new conditioned reflex. He had replaced fear with confidence.

I can hear one of my readers say, "It sounds too easy." I can only retort, "Try it for two weeks." Do not judge the technique before you use it.

Very few realize that their attitude toward themselves is reflected onto other people. If you have faith in yourself, others will have faith in you. Your personal concept of yourself goes a long way in determining your actions and behaviour.

Haven't you ever heard someone say that he isn't good at mathematics, that he isn't a good speller, or that he can't remember names? This person convinces himself of these facts over the years and accepts them as being gospel truth. Yet, let an important prospective customer be introduced to him and he'll never forget his name. Men rarely forget the name of an attractive woman.

The good things in life can be yours if you have a truly strong motivation for achieving them. You have achieved those which you now have because of your past desire to possess them.

Haven't you actually reached certain goals that you have set for yourself up to this time? I am sure that you have. But did they represent your highest goals? You have done so because you have felt capable of handling certain jobs or situations. Now, take a step forward. Picture yourself as the individual that you secretly and truly desire to be. Start this moment to live this role. Success will come to you.

You may feel that you are a failure. Which one of us has not failed at a given task or at something in our lives? This need not be the end of living for us. Let it be a stepping stone instead. Let us try to profit by whatever mistakes we have made. Many businesses fail before they become successful. Many individuals fail in their job, marriage, education and other activities. Of course, no one likes to fail, but you can guide your own destiny. If you feel that you are at the bottom of the ladder of achievement, there is only one way to go now, and that is up.

You might say, "It's very easy to talk like that when you aren't confronted with the situation." Yes, that is true, but we can profit by what has happened to others. There is a saying that goes like this, "Experience is a dear school, but fools will learn in no other." Let that not be said of anyone reading this book. If you feel at a low ebb, make up your mind this very moment to forge ahead. Paint that magic picture of the successful person you truly desire to be.

Where there is life, there is hope. Where there is hope, there are ideals. Where there are ideals, there is progress. Where there is progress, there is success!

Have you ever wondered what aerodynamic principles are involved in the take-off and flight of an airplane? The engine of the airplane gives the airplane its forward thrust. This thrust must overcome the drag or resistance of the airplane in order for it to fly. As the airplane begins to move forward at a sufficient speed, it finally begins to rise because the air hitting the bottom of the wings causes sufficient upward motion or lift. The airplane is then controlled in flight by the elevators, rudder, and ailerons.

You might ask, "Now what has this to do with the subject at hand?" I think we can learn something from this little aviation lesson. In order for our plane to fly, it seems as though various forces of resistance must be overcome. Thrust must overcome drag, and lift must overcome gravity. We also take off into the wind to create more resistance, which finally gives us more lift.

THE MAGIC OF PAINTING MENTAL PICTURES

Once this happens we can set our course with the automatic pilot and proceed to our destination.

The greater the hurdle in life the greater the effort. But also remember that the rewards are equally as great. There seems to be a law of the universe that says in order to achieve any accomplishment, one must deal with various resistances.

If one is a farmer, he must deal with the weather and soil. He does not always have favorable conditions, yet if the desire is there he can turn a desert into a land of green pastures. It is being done today through irrigation and the will of man to see things grow. If we are aiming for a higher position, we must train ourselves to work diligently each step of the way. Yes, competition is keen, but if the job were not rewarding you would not have the "resistances" again.

Don't be afraid to envision mighty vistas. Set your sights on the pinnacle of that which you hope to achieve, and start your drive with determination and confidence. What's worth doing is worth doing well. Success has little patience with compromise.

Can we use our technique of painting mental pictures to help us in this area? Yes, we can. Let us look at these various forms of resistances as a challenge. Let us think of meeting these resistances as a game. Let us call it, "The game of life." It need not be unpleasant. We can enjoy meeting these obstacles as they create new situations for which we must channel all our energies. It is like doing a crossword puzzle or putting a jig-saw puzzle togther. Our task is before us. We approach it knowing that somehow we can put the pieces together, and, finally we do it. It is work, and yet it is relaxing and pleasurable. When the jig-saw puzzle is finally put together we throw out our chests with pride and a sense of accomplishment.

Why not adopt this mental picture in your daily work, and in your long range plans for your future. It will make life a great deal easier. Make a game out of life. Of course, you are serious about your plans and your welfare, but you can add a bit of mirth to your every day living. Why not try it? Don't be like the person who reads all the wonderful books on positive thinking and the use of the subconscious mind, and then never applies any of the information.

Put aside five or ten minutes every day for the purpose of using your mind to paint mental pictures of those things which you desire in life. See yourself in these pictures. It is a highly fruitful technique. It is a sound one that deserves further investigation. Remember how we spoke of the forefathers of our great country? They were idealists. But they knew how to implement their ideals. They had painted a picture of a land of freedom. They achieved it, for they did not despair. They lived with hope and a dream. Their dream became a reality. So can yours.

Chapter V

How to Attain Self-Confidence

ONE OF THE EASIEST ways to develop self-confidence is to develop enthusiasm for what you are doing. You will soon forget about your lack of self-confidence. You won't have the time to think about it. I am sure that you have heard about occupational therapy. The goal of such therapy is to divert the patient's mind to something productive and enjoyable. The patient loses himself, so to speak, in his endeavor. The mind does not have the time to dwell upon the negative phases of the personality involved. The patient does not have the time to absorb himself in self-pity. We can gain something from this example.

If you are always thinking about your shortcomings, the opportunities that you did not grasp, your lack of education or particular skill, and other forms of self-debasement, you will continue to be devoid of drive and initiative. Life will pass you by. One of the reasons that you have the problem of lack of self-confidence is that you are always reminding yourself about it. We have heard the saying, "Life is what you make it." Well, our character is what we make it or believe it to be. Yes, develop a new zest for living, develop a new enthusiasm for your work, your family, your marriage, and your friends. It will work wonders for you. Forget the past. Live for the future!

In the foreword of this book, I suggested that one only need enthusiasm as a basic requisite for success. It is the driving force of miracles. It is the difference between life and death. I am sure you have heard the saying "Where there is life, there is hope." This does not merely refer to the process of breathing and vegetation. It means that where there is enthusiasm and fortitude, there is hope. Have you ever heard anyone say, "He died because he had nothing to live for"?

We live in a materialistic world. The stress is to build bigger and better things. The stress is for speed, efficiency and more production. Man accomplishes remarkable achievements in all of these areas. We can now fly faster than the speed of sound. We have great productive capacity. We have achieved great strides in technology. We have harnessed the atom! Yet, how far have we gone in developing and implementing a philosophy of life that will enable man to live in harmony with himself and his neighbor? We are told a war at this time can annihilate civilization. A series of H-bomb explosions can result in a chain reaction with catastrophic and devastating results. There is no place to hide from its effects.

Man has turned to religion, philosophy, and psychology for guidance. He stands now at the crossroad of civilization. It may seem at times that international politics is ineffectual, but we go on negotiating, hoping and praying for peace on earth. We know that no one can be victorious in an Atomic War. Here, I believe, is where insight will partially help solve this dilemma.

Should we throw up our hands and say, "What's the use of living?" Of course not. Remember this is the philosophy of the pessimist, the man who has lost confidence in himself and in society. Man is taking inventory of himself. He is pausing for reflection and from this reflection will come the answer. He has been forced to ask the question, "Where are we going?" The answer seems plain. The result will be that this same force with its potential for destruction will be used instead for the benefit of all mankind.

President Eisenhower, in his peace talk before the General Assembly of the United Nations, proposed and urged that the world of nations set up an atomic laboratory to which all nations would contribute scientists, and where atomic information would be pooled for the good of all. What could be better than the family of nations working in harmony? What a wonderful world this could be! This pooling plan will eventually become a reality, for it is the only path to follow.

Perhaps you feel a lack of confidence. You have taken inventory of yourself and have come away with a feeling of despair. Perhaps you have tried to overcome your lack of confidence and have failed. Perhaps you have never tried to overcome your condition and have accepted it as being a permanent liability. If you have, now is time for reflection and positive action. It is now up to you and the way you choose to see yourself. If you look at the pessimistic side of world affairs, it can drive you to distraction. But, you can find a ray of hope in the picture and be uplifted in the thought of a bright tomorrow.

You can find a ray of hope in your own assets. You need not continue to be devoid of confidence. Harness your good points to positive thinking. Your efforts for self-improvement need not be ineffectual. Through your own insight and the implementation of positive suggestion, you will be victorious.

It sounds like a battle. It is. You are winning a battle for a favorable outlook. Have you ever heard anyone say, "It's all in the way you look at it?" There is a lesson to be learned in that saying. Stop thinking and looking at yourself as one who suffers from a lack of confidence. This thinking leads to self-destruction. In a previous chapter, I suggested that you paint the picture of the individual which you, in your mind's eye, want to be, and then portray this person. Did you do it? If you didn't, start now.

Think of yourself as the confident individual you really want to be. Throw out your chest. Take a new lease on life. Forget about what has happened. The future is as bright as you want it to be. Smile with life and life will smile with you. You can control your fate through the use of these mental pictures and positive suggestions. Again, I urge you to assimilate the wisdom of this brief lesson in politics and positive thinking. It can lead only to health, prosperity and happiness.

HOW TO ATTAIN SELF-CONFIDENCE

This week, as I was writing this chapter of the book, a news flash came over the radio. Roger Bannister, an Oxford medical student, had ended the athletic world's quest of the four-minute mile track record with a monumental effort in which he was timed at 3:59.4. He had beaten the former world record of 4:01.4 established in 1945 at Malmo, Sweden by the great runner Gunder Haegg.

Roger Bannister had urged himself to a supreme effort, to climax his spectacular performance. Here is an interesting sidelight on this story. Bannister told reporters he had not decided to go all out for the world record until fifteen minutes before the start of the race. It had rained heavily during the day and a strong wind had whipped the field. About twenty minutes before race time, the sun came out and a rainbow showed in the sky. Roger Bannister said, "This is a good luck omen. I shall try for the world's record." The rest is now history.

Roger Bannister found success and the admiration of the world at the end of a rainbow. This rainbow gave him hope, enthusiasm, and self-confidence. It was all that he needed. He had found the key to his success, and it had worked like a charm. Let me ask you, my reader, a very interesting question: Do you think this great athlete could have set this new world record that day without the rainbow?

They say, "Every cloud has a silver lining." Can you look at your present position in this light? Can you see the rainbow? If you try hard enough, you will find your pot of gold.

CHAPTER VI

How to Activate
Your Subconscious Mind

UP TO THIS POINT we have been talking about
the importance of positive thinking and how essential
this is to the attainment of success. We have been discussing what can be done on the conscious level. Now,
I should like to discuss the importance of integrating the
subconscious mind into any plan for success, for it is here
that ideas and inspirations have their beginning.

Perhaps you have never given any thought to the subconscious mind and the role it plays in directing our
lives. I should like to point out that actually it does control our destiny. Let us take the case of a person suffer-
ing from an inferiority complex. Usually, this person has
been brought up in a home where the theory existed that
children should be seen and not heard. Perhaps, there
was another child in his family who was showered with
love and attention. Somehow, the former, our case in
point, was sort of left out of things. Because of this, in
his formative years, which are the first six years of life,
he was actually conditioned to feel that he wasn't as
good as his brother or sister, or that he was unworthy of
love. And so, he develops an inferiority complex which
could stay with him the rest of his life and forever retard

his emotional growth. There are numerous circumstances which can lead a child into developing other retarding personality problems, such as being brought up in a home where the parents do not get along, or where there has been a divorce or separation. It is not necessary for me to enumerate all of the possible circumstances that can contribute to the formation of personality disorders. Those mentioned above will suffice.

Let us go back and see what happens to the child who feels inadequate. He begins his schooling. He is frightened by the competitiveness of the group. He withdraws into a shell, and he might even develop a feeling of hostility toward his teacher. He doesn't like school, his teacher, or his schoolmates. The rejection of his teacher may actually be a projection of his ambivalent feelings toward his parents. He plays by himself, rejects association with other children, and thus reinforces the formation of his inferiority complex. The parents often pass this situation off by saying that Junior is just quiet. They fail to understand it. So, our little friend is left with his problem and many times never does come out of his shell. You might say, "Why don't the parents do something about the child?" The answer is that they are not aware of the seriousness of the situation. They have their own problems. The father may be busy earning a living, the mother is busy with her social activities or with household chores. There just doesn't seem to be any time to give serious consideration to their child. The weeks roll into months and the months pass into years. Special guidance is thought of only when the child becomes delinquent, or when he is incapacitated in some way because of a now serious personality problem.

Some of you may say that something similar happened to you. What can be done about it now? Is there really any hope? My answer is yes! I would like you to look at your problem as the result of negative conditioning. We are all products of our environment. We are the product of the direct or indirect suggestions that have been given to us. We have been exposed to certain stimuli over and over again. If these stimuli have not been favorable, we develop fears, doubts, prejudices, anxieties, and a myriad of other personality disorders.

You have heard that insight and the understanding of the cause of your problem will help you in solving it. This is true, but knowing the cause does not of itself always cure the problem. You may be perfectly aware of the many circumstances that have contributed to your present condition and still not be cured. You are faced with the problem of what you can do constructively to help yourself.

If we agree that one's personality is the result of conditioning, then we can also agree on a method of forming desirable personality traits. The underlying personality is formed in the subconscious mind. A person says, "I wish I could do such and such a thing, but I just can't seem to bring myself to do it." Perhaps you would like to sing in public, but the mere thought of actually doing it is enough to bring on feelings of panic.

If we could reach the subconscious mind and condition this level of the mind, we would then be able to do whatever we truly desired. It is this level of the mind that has been hindering our progress. How can we get it to work for us? How can we implant positive suggestions of confidence? How can we rid ourselves of feelings of inferiority?

The answer lies in the reconditioning of the subconscious mind. You can get your subconscious mind to work for you. It can become your friend. It doesn't matter how long you have had your problem. You can rid yourself of it by reconditioning and instilling dynamic, forceful suggestions of confidence. There are many methods of doing this. Some work more quickly than others Some are only adaptable to certain types of persons. A method that is good for John Jones might not be good for you, or vice versa.

Let us discuss the various methods that have been used. You may be able to overcome your problem through prayer, through a public speaking course, through some type of group activity, through a change of environment, and through the use of affirmations. All of these techniques deal with the problem on a conscious level. They can help immeasurably. All these methods tend to indirectly activate the subconscious mind into a reconditioning process. We often hear of wonderful results being accomplished by them, but these techniques do not represent the quickest way of reaching the subconscious.

What then is the most direct route to the subconscious mind? The answer lies in hypnosis. Under hypnosis you can be given various dynamic suggestions by the hypnotist which must work. Under self-hypnosis you can give yourself the suggestions. We know that through hypnotic suggestions a very timid, shy and reserved individual can be told that he is the greatest orator in the world and he will proceed to give an eloquent talk before a huge audience. This would be impossible for him to accomplish in any other way.

Let us look at what happens in hypnosis. The individual is put into a near sleep. His normally argumentative consciousness is now in abeyance and he is conditioned to believe that he is the greatest orator or singer the world has ever heard. These suggestions are embedded directly into the subconscious mind. Remember, we agreed that our personality is the result of being exposed to certain stimuli. Well, under hypnosis, the suggestions of confidence are firmly impressed in the subconscious. The results are automatic. They must work. The individual becomes a product of the suggestions.

How many times do you need to be bitten by a dog to have a lasting fear of dogs? It can happen as the result of one unpleasant experience. A terrifying experience leaves its impression on the subconscious so strongly that it will result in a lasting impression. If this is so, why can't positive suggestions of confidence have a lasting impression? Why can't they go directly to the subconscious where they would be certain to take effect? Normally, unless accompanied by strong emotions, they remain on the surface, on the conscious level, and only by persistent repetition do they gradually work themselves down to the subconscious. Under hypnosis the route is much more direct. We can combine the hypnosis with enthusiasm, optimism and faith.

As with positive suggestions given on a conscious level, one of the keys of hypnosis is repetition. This reinforces the establishment of the desired condition response, but the necessary repetitions are considerably less.

I have suggested that the quickest way of attaining a new conditioned response is through hypnosis. I realize that my proposing this will not have mass appeal. You may not be familiar with hypnosis. You may have a fear of it, you may not want to be hypnotized. You may feel it is dangerous. You may feel that you will be made to do or say things you do not wish to do or say. I can assure you that your reluctance is unfounded. Hypnotism is now being used extensively in psychotherapy as a means of helping people. There has also been a recent move by dentists to use it in their work to eliminate fear and pain.

Everyone of us is suggestible; some more than others. Hypnosis merely implies that a heightened state of suggestibility is induced. There is nothing to fear. It employs a normal characteristic of personality. We have been discussing positive suggestions during this entire book. The favorable response to these suggestions is determined by your suggestibility and willingness to accept the positive affirmations that we have proposed. I am therefore suggesting that we use a hypnotic technique so that we can make better use of these same conscious suggestions. Should this technique not appeal to you, do not use it. Our other methods based on a conscious integration of suggestions will work as well, but not as quickly.

For those of you who would like to use this technique, I have outlined an actual procedure that you can use to reach and activate your subconscious mind. If you carefully follow the instructions, you will be pleasantly surprised.

CHAPTER VII

The Techniques of Reaching Your Subconscious Mind

I HAVE GIVEN DETAILED instruction for attaining self-hypnosis in several of my other books. I shall outline here in detail another technique that you can use effectively. The goal, of course, is to reach a highly suggestible state in which you will be able to implant positive suggestions in your subconscious mind. As a result of these suggestions, you will instill a new conditioned reflex. The same stimuli will take on different responses. In the case of the person who could not give a speech before the group, hypnosis instilled in his subconscious mind the suggestions that he could. When this was accomplished the same stimulus of the group had a favorable response. So we see once again that it is necessary to reach the subconscious mind to instill suggestions of confidence.

I have often been asked, "How long will it take before I am able to see results?" This, of course, is impossible to answer. Every case is different, since no two people have ever been exposed to the exact same experiences. I have seen miraculous results in a short period of time, and I have seen progress only after a long duration of time. What then is the factor that determines the progress of this therapy or the progress of any other method of therapy? It is up to you! I can give you the technique to be used. I can point out step by step what to do, but I cannot do it for you.

Your enthusiasm and motivation for change are factors that only you can control. You may have heard a doctor say, "I cannot do anything else for the patient. It is up to the patient now if he is to get well. If he wants to get well, he will." You might say, "Everyone wants to be well." Yes, this is true in a sense, but often the "illness" is the only means of a person's getting attention. It may give him a sense of importance. I am sure that you know people who get sick when they cannot have their own way, or when they want to avoid an unpleasant task.

If the sickness takes on the form of a conditioned response, the person can find himself trapped by it. That is, the sickness becomes an unconscious result of certain stimuli. We are all prone to it, and no one is infallible, including the psychologist. If we understand it, though, we are better able to cope with it and effect a cure for it. Everyone has problems. The difference between people lies in the manner in which they are able to cope with their problems. One person's problem gives him a nervous breakdown; another is able to deal with the same problem in a logical and self-assuring manner.

We have already agreed that it is desirable to reach the subconscious mind. Now, how do we go about doing it? Before I tell you this, I should like to point out certain things about the subconscious mind and the way it works. We know that when we fall asleep the subconscious level of the mind takes control of the bodily functions. The subconscious mind seems to have an intelligence of its own. It keeps us from rolling off the bed and it is alert at all times. Our dreams stem from the subconscious mind. It is also the reservoir of all that we have ever learned. Once conditioned, it will respond in the same manner every time unless reconditioned.

Set aside ten minutes every day for the following technique, which I suggest you try when you are about to fall asleep at night. You are in bed, the lights are out, and you are ready to fall asleep. Some of you may fall asleep immediately; others may turn and toss for quite a long time. Incidentally, this technique will help those of you who are unable to fall asleep immediately. Now, begin by giving yourself mental suggestions of relaxation. Our purpose is to reach a state where you are just about to fall asleep. This is the highly desirable state where we find an interaction of the conscious and subconscious mind. Our task now is to give ourselves mentally whatever suggestions we desire. Even should you fall asleep while doing this, do not despair for the suggestions will carry over into the subconscious mind.

It is desirable to learn to control this state. This state is very similar to that of slowly waking up when you are dreaming. You are awake and yet you are aware that you are dreaming. This is an example of the interaction of the conscious and subconscious mind. If you desire, you can wake up during this dream-awake period or you can fall back to sleep to continue your dream. I am sure that some of you have interrupted a dream for some reason and then gone back to bed to finish the dream. This is not too uncommon. It shows excellent control of your subconscious. Can you wake up whenever you desire without an alarm clock? If you can, you will find quick results from this technique. You also have good control of your subconscious. You have noticed that I have told you to give yourself the various suggestions that you desire mentally. You need not repeat these aloud, they will be just as effective when done silently.

The technique sounds simple enough, doesn't it? I urge my readers to try it for two weeks. You will be amazed at what it can do for you. You have the opportunity of molding your future. It is up to you. Remember the following adage, "You can lead a horse to water, but you can't make him drink." I have presented to you those factors that have helped countless individuals to attain a rich and rewarding life. We all have the same capacity for success, but some of us never reach out for it. The decision is now yours. I hope that you will apply some of the principles that we have discussed.

Most people will be able to see some tangible results within a short period. Use the suggestions every night. Couple this with the other material that we have discussed in this book about positive thinking.

CHAPTER VIII

Lady Luck Can Smile on You

UP TO THIS POINT I have been proposing various techniques of utilizing positive thinking. Whatever technique you use, the results will be the same. You will find success, because you are on the right road to success. It will take some longer than others. This is to be expected, but everyone will achieve his goal. Do not judge your progress by others. No two people have the same background.

A man attending one of my lectures expressed the belief that success in life was merely a matter of getting the right breaks and opportunities. He said that if one were lucky, he would become successful, if not, he wouldn't. He went on to explain that he didn't give much credence to the idea of positive thinking. His philosophy was that Lady Luck is on your side, or she is not. Here was a disillusioned individual. Nothing that I could say would change his mind. He had accepted as his inevitable fate the conviction that "Lady Luck" was not with him. After my lecture, I had coffee and cake with this gentleman at one of the tables that were provided in the social hall. I found it impossible to change his point of view. Unfortunately this man had lost his zest for living. He had been on the same job for twenty-five years and had not advanced in his work or in his mental development.

I felt truly sorry for him. If only he could have been as resolute in feeling that Lady Luck was on his side, he would have achieved his goal in life. Even now as I think about him, I cannot help but wonder why he came to listen to my lecture in the first place. The announcement clearly indicated that I was going to talk on the importance of positive thinking. Was he really looking for help? Had I failed him? Somehow, I had failed to stir his imagination. It is, of course, extremely difficult to undo in an hour's lecture the negative conditioning of a lifetime, although there is success in many instances in fostering a desire to further investigate this subject of positive thinking.

An essential factor in the use of positive thinking is motivation. One must have the desire to advance himself. If not, a thousand lectures will not change his mind. This motivation must come from within.

Over the years, I have taught numerous courses in the art of positive thinking. I have seen wonderful results in both young and old men and women. I have seen disillusioned and seemingly hopeless persons become self-assured and confident individuals. With these individuals though, and with the many others, there was a common denominator.

They had the motivation to change. The rest was comparatively easy. For several months, they filled their minds with only positive thoughts. When former students visited in class, they spoke of their negative thinking in the past and told how they saw themselves in retrospect for perhaps the first time. After this, though, it was a matter of looking toward the future. Many of the stories were inspiring ones and they lent moral support to those who were going through a re-conditioning process.

I would like to tell you the story of one student of positive thinking. This young man was twenty-nine years old, and had a bad case of inferiority. He had come out to Los Angeles from Chicago as he felt the change would do him good. He took the first job that came along and had worked at it for four years without a single raise in salary. One evening he came to class early to discuss his personal problem. He had met a young lady, had fallen in love, and wanted to get married, but felt he could not do it on his present salary. I asked him if he were due for a raise shortly and he then told me that he had never had a raise in pay since he had started the job. This was the crucial moment to test the validity of our theory of positive thinking.

I suggested that he ask his employer for a raise. He gave me a thousand excuses why he couldn't. The boss was an impossible person with whom to deal in matters like this. He had turned down many others and this young man didn't want to be subjected to the same embarrassment. I asked him if he really felt he was worth more money at his job. If he did, that was all that was necessary. He replied in the affirmative. Finally, we both agreed that he would speak to his boss and explain to him why he felt that a raise was justified. Within the next six months our friend received not one raise, but two very substantial ones. This young man asserted himself for perhaps one of the very few times in his life. The last time I heard from him he told me that he had been made production manager of the plant. Oh yes, I did attend his wedding and met his lovely bride.

This young man in our true story needed only a little guidance together with some positive thinking and some one on his side rooting for him. Everyone of us can use proper guidance at some time during our life time. Many of us are reluctant to seek it. We look upon it as a sign of weakness. Many a marriage could be saved if only the couple would seek the help of a competent marriage counselor. Many a delinquent child could be saved as well.

The other important factor in our story is that this young man had the love of his sweetheart. He wanted to make good for her. This was the motivation that first brought him to see me. There is no greater motivation on earth than the love of a woman. She was rooting for him. I was there to lend him moral support as well. It was as though we were the cheering section. Can you visualize a football game without a rooting section or fans in the stadium? I can, but I'm afraid the players would be lacking in enthusiasm. There is nothing as good for the morale as to know that others are on your side, cheering for your victory.

Did Lady Luck suddenly decide to smile on our friend? I am afraid that I can not concur with such a thought. I adhere to the theory that one must proceed in a logical manner to make Lady Luck smile on him. It need not happen to the next fellow all the time. Search yourself. What have you done lately to feel the warm rays of Lady Luck? If you have done nothing, then my advice is to begin this very moment to bring about favorable changes. Reading this book is one of the first steps in that direction. I trust I have given you some inspiration and hope.

Remember, it will not do you any good to read this book or any other book on positive thinking, agree with its contents, and then put it aside to return to your old ways.

This is the challenge for everyone. We all realize that it is not any easy task, but we all know that it can be done. It requires a little fortitude, motivation and faith. If you really want to advance yourself, you can. It requires work. You may become disheartened, but do not despair. It is easier than you believe it to be. Once you begin using positive thinking, a new world will open up for you, and Lady Luck will smile on you.

Have you ever heard Jimmy Durante sing the song, "You Got To Start Off the Day With a Song?" There is wisdom in this title and in the rest of the words of the song. Let me give you a tip that has helped many to achieve success. Take the advice of the song. Start the day with a song, with a smile, with gratitude that you can be productive. Don't be the fellow that dreads to face the day. Every day can be a rewarding experience.

CHAPTER IX

The Secret of Achieving Success

IF SUCCESS IS TO COME TO YOU, you must do your part to encourage it. All through this book we have been talking about success and how to achieve it. In doing this, we must remember to practice the golden rule. All religions teach us to do unto others as we would have them do unto us. There is a sound psychological basis for this tenet. In practice this philosophy will do wonders for you. You can achieve success without hurting anyone in the process. The individual who achieves his goal at the expense of someone else's welfare has achieved nothing. Success must have a spiritual counterpart or it is void.

Success in life should never be sought for selfish reasons. You must have charity in your heart. It is not enough to practice the golden rule at the holiday season only. It must be a part of your life. Don't practice brotherhood only for brotherhood week. Make it a part of your daily living. I am suggesting that an important phase of having Lady Luck smile on you is to practice your religion. I do not necessarily mean that you must attend services. I mean rather that you should live a truly spiritual life in your daily routine. Yes, the majority of the successful people I know do lead rich spiritual lives.

People have been able to do wonders for themselves through the medium of prayer. It is an infallible means of arousing and tapping your inward power. Through prayer, one comes to see only the good in life. It is through prayer that one visualizes himself as healthy, successful, and courageous. Man's noblest aspirations have their origin in prayer. If one prays wholeheartedly, all his prayers will be answered.

I spoke of successful men leading rich spiritual lives. You may say you know someone who does not lead a spiritual life, yet is extremely successful. This man must have faith, or he would never be where he is today. He might not talk of his faith, but I can assure you that he has a creed, or he could never have aroused within himself those forces that led to his success.

The miserly Ebenezer Scrooge, in the Charles Dicken's story of Tiny Tim, never found happiness in his vast accumulation of wealth until he shared it with the family of his struggling clerk, Bob Cratchit. It was only then he found that life had a spiritual meaning. Up to then he had been leading a meaningless existence.

The Congress of the United States has just set aside a special room for meditation and prayer. Certainly we can all follow its example. The slogan that was used last year by all religious groups to foster church attendance reads, "A family that prays together, stays together." Doesn't this make a beautiful picture? There must be harmony in this setting. The individuals of such a group will find peace of mind. And this is the best stepping stone to success. A man or woman living in a harmonious environment cannot help but find his mark in life.

Without hope, man is devoid of drive. Without faith, man is devoid of initiative. The greatest teachings of all time have come from men of God. If we only would follow their wisdom what a wonderful world this would be for all people! As we become older, we become more spiritual. We search our souls for the meaning of life. We search our souls and question what we have done in life. We all seek peace of mind. We ask ourselves, "What have I done for my fellow human beings?" "Have I been charitable?" I do not necessarily mean in monetary ways. You can be charitable by giving a kind word, by helping someone with a problem, by lending a helping hand. The prophets tell us one of the greatest forms of charity is to help someone find employment so that he may become self-sufficient.

If you have thought only of yourself in all your endeavors, yours is the wrong road. It is a bumpy road that will never lead to any real satisfaction. I call your attention once again to all the successful people who give freely of their time and services for charitable causes. They don't have to contribute, but they are eager to lend a hand.

I used to spend my summers in Northern Maine. Sometimes at night, I would climb the surrounding mountains. The sky was luminous and clear, and I felt that I could reach out and touch the stars. It gave me a majestic feeling. The scene was conducive to reflection. It was conducive to self-evaluation. I felt that I, as well as all other men, was a part of this vast intricate design of Mother Nature. The question was raised in my mind, "What am I doing with this precious life that has been given to me?" "Am I making the most of it?" We can all strive for better things, not only for ourselves but for society as a whole.

May I suggest at this point that you take the time to indulge in a period of meditation and self-examination. Most people never do this because they keep themselves so busy. I think it is good for the soul. I have suggested it to you, as I feel very strongly that it is a very important factor in attaining success.

Hard work alone is not the answer for success. Someone once said, "There never was a successful business where there was no laughter." I know individuals who have labored diligently at their chosen fields and never found any real success at them. I honestly believe that part of the explanation of their failure is that they are too materialistic. They lack the leaven of spirituality. When I have suggested this to them, they scoffed at the very idea of it. Each man, of course, is entitled to his own belief.

I am thinking of the story of a man who did not believe in God and no amount of argument could change his mind. This man's only son had become ill, and the doctor advised him that his chances of survival were negligible. This, of course, came to the father as a great shock and here for the first time, he turned to God and prayed that his son should live.

It is better to live with faith than without it. It will make one's life beautiful and rewarding. It is the foundation of happiness, harmony and success.

Standing shoulder to shoulder with spiritual faith, as a factor of success, is the principle of faith in yourself. There is perhaps no greater force in the sphere of human endeavor than that which emanates from one's faith in himself. The instances of attaining success without it are so rare as to be virtually non-existent. Faith is a vast and enduring source of assurance whence comes the drive so vitally an incident of achievement. Once you believe in yourself and what you are seeking to accomplish, you will generate a force which will drive you to a successful attainment of your goal. Without it, you lack the necessary strength and sustenance to bring about the results you seek. Not only is faith a highly potent and influential stimulant in generating your own attitude and power of fulfillment, but it will cause others to have faith in you. Faith has a vividly unique quality of radiation which reaches out to embrace all those with whom you come into contact. If you believe in yourself, others will believe in you; if you despair and lament your own lack of confidence, you may be sure there will be plenty to endorse your platform of incompetence. Reach into your own circle of acquaintances, segregate the successes from the failures, and eventually you will conclude that the men and women who have reached their goal did so by treading the staunch highway of faith in themselves. There is a brilliant luster to the quality of faith which shines and glistens prosperously with the assurance of accomplishment. It is an immediate signal to all who happen within the broad beams of its rays to make way for a potentially successful man.

That faith in yourself which generates an immediate response in others is readily demonstrated in the broad example of the comedian dedicated to the entertainment of patrons who pay an admission price to laugh. There is perhaps no more hard-crusted group of people in the world than those who constitute an audience defying someone to make them laugh. The performer who has faith in himself takes immediate control of the situation. He is assured and infectious. The audience responds at once, regarding him with the same confidence he feels in himself. He has destroyed the barrier of their skepticism and softened them to a degree where they are no longer challenging him to provoke their laughter, but are eager and willing to encourage him to continue by laughter which, on occasion, may not even be warranted. Faith and assurance have turned the trick, and this man has succeeded.

The opposite is true of the man who addresses his audience with little faith in himself and his material. The patrons are quick to sense it; he has transmitted nothing to inspire their confidence; and he is usually greeted with such reticence that he is constantly waging a combat with those who could, if suitably impressed, issue his passport to success. This, of course, pertains not only to the comedian, but the performer or artist in each of the numerous categories of entertainment.

Closely annexed to the quality of faith, and an invariable outgrowth of this essential endowment, is another prime factor to success—authority. Authority in an individual to effectively permeate his sphere of influence need not be charged with a quality of overt or demonstrative force, but is, rather, a subtle force which normally emanates from the individual's fund of self-confidence. The individual who is deeply confident in himself, in his ability to achieve that which he has set out to do, will radiate a certain invasive influence which will inspire others to have confidence in him. Authority has always had a certain connotation of power of fulfillment.

The badge of the police officer is an emblem of authority resident in the man to carry out the powers delegated to him by the police power; the credentials of the health inspector are his delegated authority from the Board of Health to enforce the measures provided for public therapy; the elaborate resources set up to enforce the decree of a judge or a magistrate, constitute a manifestation of the authority delegated to him to adjudicate the controversial issues involved in conflict within the social order.

We are quick to recognize and respect this authority.

It represents to us an implied power in each of these individuals to accomplish that which challenges their prerogative. We feel confident that these people are equipped to do whatever is necessary to a successful consummation of the purposes to which they have devoted themselves, and we are conditioned to respond accordingly. It is nothing more than that their facilities for achievement have set up an authority in them to which we react by confidence in them that they can actually do what their emblem of authority says they can do.

Let your faith and self-confidence be your badge of authority to induce others to confidence in you. If you really believe in yourself and the purposes to which you have dedicated yourself, or propose to dedicate yourself, and entertain a conviction of assurance about your ability for their accomplishment, others will readily recognize that you are equipped with the necessary facilities for enforcement. You will have taken a giant stride in the direction of your eventual success.

In all discussions pertaining to success, it would be singularly remiss to skirt, or avoid, any mention of another essential ingredient to its accomplishment— perseverance. Perseverance and tenacity are such proven essentials that it is not only difficult but impossible to contemplate success without them. You may have a faith in yourself and your ability to achieve a certain purpose. This, in turn, will serve to ignite the fuel of confidence, which, in turn, will generate and radiate the

heat of authority to alert others to your resourcefulness to accomplish what you propose to do. So far you
are well on your way and success appears imminent.
Rest assured that not only is there no imminence about
your success, but its realization is doomed to destruction without that all-essential factor of perseverance.
I know not whom I quote for so many are they who
in their wisdom have uttered the prophetic words,
"Perseverance is the price of success." Stick to it. If you
have a purpose, a resolution, a promise to yourself, anything which you have decided to successfully accomplish, stick to it. Don't be swayed from your course by
anything short of an honest conviction in your heart
and in your mind that what you have set out to do is
wrong for you.

There is no disgrace in erring. It is distinctly human
to err. If, at a given point in your pursuit of success,
you can honestly tell yourself you have chosen the
wrong path, by all means save valuable time and energy
by making a detour, but be convinced that what you
are relinquishing is the result of wise and careful judgment, and not the result of lack of perseverance.

Nothing in this world comes easily. In spite of what
occasional evidence you have seen to the contrary, nothing worth while does come easily. Don't rely upon the
meager and rare exceptions to this irrefutable truth.
Wishing doesn't accomplish it; waiting doesn't accomplish it; a miracle might accomplish it, but inventory
the list of miracles in your stock of human experiences,

and I doubt if you'll place much faith in that phenomenon for accomplishment. The rule is virtually invariable: Only doing will accomplish, and in doing it you must persevere. The result of unalterable perseverance is assured success.

Don't be swayed by others. Nine times out of ten they will, upon investigation, be revealed as people who themselves have never persisted at anything until its ultimate consummation. Many of us have all the necessary attributes for becoming a success, but-are plagued by one insidious obstruction. We are easily discouraged, especially in the face of imposing obstacles.

What success can exist without obstacles? The very term "success," in its popular conception, contemplates the act of transcending obstacles. Every "success" story is predicated on the theme of surmounting obstacles, encountering conflict, and effectively combating it. Think back to the last play you saw, a recent movie, a novel, or the autobiography or biography of a famous individual. Why did it interest you? Why was it good? What held the audience? Conflict. Ninety times out of a hundred, the interesting device employed by the author was conflict. Whether it be emotional, physical or mental, the basic foundation of the story, the cement upon which was founded the structure, was conflict. Why was the situation interesting, absorbing or suspenseful? For a very good reason. Conflict is realism. It is a circumstance which has been prominently involved in everyone's lifetime, not once, but many, many times—in fact,

probably every time the person sought to accomplish
something out of the ordinary.

Every effort toward accomplishment is refuted or
thwarted or repelled somewhere along the line. In de-
feating the obstacle the way is cleared for its achievement, and once the barriers have been kicked aside, success in that particular endeavor is inevitable. The situation in your book, play or movie was interesting for
another reason. Everyone admires success. They like to
see people accomplish things. But they place no value
on accomplishment attained without conflict—without
barriers. They recognize that there can be no success
in the true sense of the word without it, but once it
exists, once there is real conflict, and once it has been
destroyed to pave the road to success, they are satisfied
and happy—satisfied because the requirements of realism have been met; happy because the achievement
through difficulty pleases them. Once you have
recognized your conflict and persevered to the successful destruction of your obstacles, you will have achieved
success in its true form.

Remember the axiom: Nothing succeeds like success.
It has become a thread-bare cliche with excessive usage,
but it is true. If it weren't it wouldn't be nearly as over-
worked as it is. Stick to your guns! Persevere! If you
don't meet obstacles, what you are after is not worth
fighting for. When you do meet them, you have encountered conflict—an ingredient in every success story.
Perseverance will ultimately resolve your conflict, and

you will come out of the fray victorious—a success by every standard in the meticulous gauge of notable accomplishment.

To avoid any ambiguity in our thinking on this point, permit me to underscore a further essential observation. Perseverance is too often dissipated, to a degree of becoming virtually ineffectual, by being employed in too many diverse undertakings at the same time. As previously pointed out, ambition, energy and drive are not only highly commendable qualities, but extremely essential to the attainment of success. However, as with anything else, when these factors are forced to encompass numerous projects, rather than a single purpose, they will not function at full strength. Anything which is required to cover a broad surface will spread thin. Don't let this happen to your perseverance.

Success is difficult enough to accomplish when your facilities are all directed in a single channel to a principal target. You can't afford to reduce the efficiency of your ammunition by reducing its full force and impact. The result is bound to become one of those deplorable situations in which you are directing feeble punches at several opponents, rather than a knockout blow at one victim. Your heart will ride on every thrust, but none will contain enough drive for that all-important Sunday punch. You will eventually be forced to relinquish some of your projects for lack of energy, and inevitably you will be tripping over the loose ends of your unfinished enterprises.

THE SECRET OF ACHIEVING SUCCESS

Tackle one objective at a time. Tackle with your heart, your ambition, your energy, and all your might. One defeated opponent is worth a dozen half-beaten ones. Once a project has been successfully accomplished, you will derive from it additional strength to combat your next one. Like an army utilizing the strength of its captives to the accomplishment of its objective, so will you each time harness the power of your achievements in striking out at other objectives. But hit your objectives singly, with full power and avail yourself of its crushing impact. Succeed by all means, but take your measure of success in stride—a step at a time. Set your sights, no matter how distant and broad your ultimate horizon, and then, persevere until you achieve it. Perseverance will do it, but bear in mind that perseverance is a physical manifestation of your mental conviction. Without the mental impulse, the overt physical deed will not occur. Therefore, by logical and irrefutable deduction, the positive thought is completely essential to generate the machinery. Think positively and you will positively do.

There is an additional factor worthy of comment in any treatise which embraces a comprehensive consideration of the subject of success—health. At this point you might well, and with justification, ask the questions, "Is there no end to the list of requirements? Why must all these ingredients be employed to achieve success? Are not a few carefully selected factors sufficient if employed to the fullest degree of their utility?" The answer, unfortunately, is that a few factors will not suffice. All the forces of accomplishment must be utilized to engage the enemy, which in this case is failure. Would you send half a team out on the gridiron to engage a formidable opponent? Would you disperse with a couple of outfielders, a shortstop and a third baseman against a strong opponent on the baseball diamond? Would you relinquish one flank of your army in combat against a powerful foe on the battlefield? Of course you wouldn't. What would be your chance of success? Virtually none. I have in each instance suggested that the opposition is an imposing one. The reason for this is purposeful, because obstacles to success always take the field at full strength. Like a highly skilled, carefully coordinated team, each man a specialist in his position, and all units functioning as one, each implementing the vigor of the other, each according to the other the strength of his own resourcefulness, all the factors of success are interrelated and must unite to face the common foe with a solid front, in waging the battle for victory. Vitally a part of this offensive unit, ingeniously formed to keep the entire machinery of production operating at top efficiency, is the health link in our gold chain of success. Again we refer to the athlete in exemplifying our point. Not that other examples might not aptly demonstrate what the author wishes to convey, but because the case of the athlete, and his relationship to the success of the team is so singularly parallel to the function of each unit in our own overall pattern of success.

Assume that eleven men have been selected to form a football team. Each man has rigidly disciplined him-

self and carefully directed all his facilities toward the
epitome of skill and accomplishment in his particular
function on the team. Each position represents a gold
link in our success chain. The ends represent faith, the
guards, confidence, the tackler, assurance, the center,
authority, the backs, perseverance, and the other factors
we have listed. If each unit reaches top efficiency, success is inevitable. Each signal called by the quarterback
immediately alerts each cog as to what its next operation must be to successfully make a gain in the direction of its ultimate goal. There is no time to stop and
ponder the decision as to what to do. The operation is
skilled to the degree of being virtually mechanical. Each
man takes his cue at once and the forward motion is
begun and propelled by each wheel in the machine. But
now, during the training period, one man—one link—
has become careless. He feels that since all of the other
links are strong and accomplished, he can afford to let
down. A few drinks, late hours, incorrect diet and sleep-
less nights begin to take their toll. His thinking process
slows down. Alertness eludes him. But still he doesn't
worry, because each of the other links is equipped to
execute the play.

Then comes the day of the big game—the battle
for success. He fails, and the others fail with him. He
zigs when he should have zagged. By being out of position, too slow, inaccurate, lacking in stamina, he throws
the entire team out of balance. All of the other facets
of production which relied upon him to do his part, in
order to effectively enable them to do their own jobs,

find they cannot depend upon him. The assurance they feel about their own function is dissipated to the extent of their anxiety about him. Efficiency is accordingly diminished, and the charge to success bogs down.

In preparing for your own success, it is essential that you subject yourselves to the strictest rules of personal hygiene. You must go into training, just as must the athlete. Your teammates, which are all the other implements to success, are reliant upon the factor of good health. Do not let them down. Good health is the vital generator that propels power to all of the other factors. Without that fuel they cannot perform their specialized tasks of offensive plays toward the goal of success. Good health will supply all the necessary force of momentum, provided, of course, the other factors are prepared to utilize their delegation of power.

Nothing written here is intended to exclude from success those of you who are the innocent victims of various unavoidable afflictions. Countless are those who have achieved success by overcoming such impairments as loss of limbs, eyesight, hearing, injury to the spine or various essential organs, and numerous other misfortunes. Their credit will be all the greater for overcoming them.

The examples are too numerous to mention, and, I am sure, immediately present themselves to you. As previously mentioned, the example of Franklin D. Roosevelt, regardless of your political leanings, is probably one that is more than a little worthy of note in this connection. A diligent application of the other factors essential to success will compensate for whatever of these impairments exist in your own case. But the important point I make here is that regardless of your physical and mental make-up, you must, to achieve success, protect what you have by giving it every benefit of good health. It is God-given; defend it with every reverence that you would accord any other sacred endowment. Observe this consideration diligently and you will have tremendously amplified and fortified your task force of success.

CHAPTER X

Attaining Financial Security

EVERY NEW IDEA, somewhere along the line, will be met with either indifference or skepticism. There is an ingrained reluctance on the part of most people to accept new things. Samuel Morse had his telegraphic equipment turned down by Congress. The reason? No practical value! Thomas Edison found a great deal of resistance in having his electric light bulb accepted because he had had neither formal education nor scientific standing. People scoffed at the idea of being able to talk through a hollow wire, as the telephone was called in its early days. Who now can even think of modern living without a telephone?

These men, these inventors had something in common and that was a resourcefulness, an ingenuity, and a deep faith in their own ability to reproduce their dream. They had hope and enthusiasm. They had to struggle long and hard but they never considered giving up. They had the will to win. If you have a sincere desire to better yourself you will do it as surely as you are reading this book. Nothing can stop you.

There is an unlimited market for a good product. The success of your product may lie in your enthusiasm for it. You must honestly believe in its value. This type of thinking is contagious. The person who you are trying to interest in the product will sense the sincerity of your representations. Many times this can be the factor which will determine whether or not a product is given further thought or consideration. Your presentation of the product or idea should be given a great deal of thought for it is most important. Remember . . . be enthusiastic about it. If you are not, you cannot expect that the prospective customer will be excited about it either.

There is no saturation point for new services, talents, ideas or products. Little more than a decade ago there were few people who could conceive of the idea that most families in large cities would have their own television sets. But then, almost overnight, a new market was created and its product supplied into the homes of millions. A new world of entertainment and enlightenment was born. It was a blessing for invalids and other shut-ins as well as for all those who wanted to be entertained at home.

Home builders are always dreaming up new ideas to entice people to buy their particular homes rather than those of their competitors. Real estate competition is keen and it is usually the one offering the best and most attractive home at the most reasonable price who gets the sale. Some friends of mine who were really interested in giving the public a "good deal" so to speak, believed this to be true. They decided to be builders. They had had no experience, but they went ahead with a survey of the houses being offered by others. They decided that many features were being left out of low priced homes that could be included without lessening the margin of profit to be made. They were told by the best building authorities, this was not true, and that it could not be done. But this did not stop them. They hired a group of architects and told them what they wanted. Seven model homes were built and within two months they had sold two hundred. Amazing isn't it? The secret was in imagination, vision and the actual giving of real value at a reasonable price.

Another home builder in Midwest City, Oklahoma, had a truly ingenious idea. His problem was similar to that of all builders. What could he do to make his homes more attractive than those of his competitors? All the houses were fairly similar, and sold at comparable prices. One day the idea came to him. He would give a pony free to each family buying one of his houses. These houses were built primarily for young couples with children. What greater delight could a child have than to own his own pony? This builder decided that he would build a community stable for the ponies. His idea caught on like wild fire. When the parents could not quite make up their minds as to which home to buy the children helped consummate the deal. I need not tell you what good salesmen children can be when they really want something. As a result, the social life of the community became well integrated around this innovation. I need mention only a few side effects. The children have been given a new and wonderful sense of responsibility. Parents have little or no problem of discipline. What child wouldn't drink his milk when he knew that in another five minutes or so he could be out riding his pony with the rest of his playmates?

Anyone could have thought of this idea. I can assure you that many will borrow it now. It took the foresight of one man, a man who himself, as a child, had always wanted a Shetland pony, but had never gotten one. Like this example, most workable ideas need not be complicated. Most require merely the adding of a new twist to an old idea. Our job may be to find a new use for things we already have. The builder in our last example did this. Another builder whose homes were not moving too well decided to build a community swimming pool. Almost immediately his houses were sold.

I maintain that this idea of adding something new, or of giving a new twist to an existent product, or a new use can be applied to almost every line of endeavor. Patience is required—and thought. Give your mind plenty of time to dwell on your particular problem and its possible solutions. Work on it every day. Answers will come to you. It is usually best to confine yourself to those fields with which you are already familiar. Here your experience is naturally greater and experience itself has an enormous value.

The development and implementation of your ideas will obtain financial security for you in the normal course of events. But the immediate goal should not be financial. It should be that of perfecting your service, idea or product.

Do you have a favorite singer? Why do you like him? It is probably because you like his or her style of singing. The popular singers of today develop curiously individual styles of tone production, phrasing, sound modulation and gesturing. They try for different interpretations of rhythms. None of these happen accidentally. Singers work at developing and perfecting their techniques. Should the public like the end results they are made. Their success is assured.

What about the thousands of talented performers who are never successful? Here in Hollywood, the talent capital of the world, you meet many such individuals. Here competition is incredibly keen. Always there are some performers explaining that they are waiting for a lucky break. This is precisely what is wrong. No one can wait for a lucky break. One must always go after it. Personally, I do not believe in a theory of success that would have you waiting idly for a lucky break, a break that may never come. One should be aggressive in every field. Never sit back and wait for things to shape themselves. They won't.

We cannot deny the fact that people sometimes do get lucky breaks that lead to success. But remember that you must have your ability developed as they did when opportunity knocked, or the chance will slip away. Instead of waiting idly for the break, prepare yourself for the time when you will be able to take advantage of it. If you seriously work toward this goal, what you call the "breaks" will certainly come to you. You will make your own. Remember that what is a lucky break to one person may not be so to another. It is all a matter of interpretation. Look at every opportunity as a luck break, and each will serve as a stepping stone to success and financial security.

We know that since the end of World War II there has been an emphasis upon distribution rather than on production. Along with this there has been greater importance given the individual salesman who finally makes the sale. During the war years one needed only to produce and the product was sold. With the curtailment of government spending and the return to normal competition the man in the selling field took on increased stature. His is a vital job in a peacetime economy. Anyone interested in the selling field today need not wait for a lucky break. All companies can use the services of good salesmen. A company's success is in a large degree dependent upon its selling staff and the caliber of the men that comprise it. I know companies that turn out wonderful products, but never quite attain success, because they lack an aggressive sales forces. Someone in the concern may take up the cry that business is slow and very quickly the sales force can be caught in the web. They come to feel that there is no use trying to really sell, and for that concern it soon is all over. This may seem an over-simplification but in essence this is what really happens.

No one can deny that we are living in a land of opportunity. It may be true that business as a whole is not as good as it has been during the last ten years. But there seem to be those companies that do well during all periods. Is there a secret to it? I don't think so. I think it is nothing more, than the philosophy of positive thinking and positive action being put into actual practice.

We all experience frustrating days and periods. However, these need not hamper our progress. We should try to take them in stride and continue in our vein of positive thinking. If our judgment proves incorrect we shall, of course, be somewhat disappointed. But no one is entirely free from making wrong decisions, and though these wrong decisions may be costly they need not mean the end of hope or life. It is a good practice when you find that you have made a wrong decision or acted foolishly to admit it first to yourself and then to those concerned. At first we may find this difficult but it actually does make for easier living. It is a mature person who can realize his mistakes and take a lesson from them. Having made this admission, tackle the problem or situation with new vigor and determination, and you will find that nothing is really as bad as it seems. Financial success like any other accomplishment requires work, discipline, insight and the exercising of creative ability.

If a man is to be succesful, he must stick to his goal and not become discouraged at every little setback. He should have a long range objective as well as an immediate one lined up for himself. Lasting success rarely comes overnight. Many people tend to forget this, but it continues to be true.

There should be pride in work, no matter what kind

it is. We cannot all be lawyers, doctors and executives nor should we all want to be. But we can all take pride in our own kind of work, and find success in the field to which we have devoted ourselves. The high living standard of the United States is the result of dynamic, aggressive positive thinking people. These people are interested in change, in improvement, in the endless betterment of our way of life. They dream and make their dream a reality. And so can we, . . . all of us. For these leaders and innovators are not born with markedly special attributes. They court success and they do it in the manner outlined in this book.

It Is All Up to You

YOU HAVE ALREADY read the importance of positive thinking, the magic of painting mental pictures, how to attain self-confidence, how to activate and reach your subconscious mind, and other contributing factors that lead to success. The problem which now presents itself is how to begin to implement these findings.

You might say, "These things that you have pointed out in your book sound fine, but can I really apply the power of positive thinking to my own case?" My answer once again is yes! You can certainly emulate the successful people who have used this power. You need only begin.

We have come to a very critical point in our discussion. It is time to put into practice that which you have learned. For some reason it is always a difficult task to stir from the inertia to which one has become accustomed. Here is the challenge, though, that one must face. If he accepts it and acts upon it, success will surely come.

Try to direct your energies along lines that suit your inclinations or particular talents. Keep constantly in your mind the picture of the successful person that you want to be. Try to avoid negative thoughts, and do not discuss your shortcomings or the unpleasant experiences that have happened to you.

Do you know people who start to tell you all their troubles just as soon as you meet them? They are constantly lamenting their problems. They never seem to get out of their dilemma. One unpleasant experience after another seems to befall them. If you happen to be one of these unfortunate individuals, take my advice . . . stop telling the world your troubles! People have their own problems. If you really want help, seek the help and guidance of a competent counselor.

It is always desirable, of course, to talk about your new goals and aspirations. The repetition will firmly implant these ideas both in your conscious and subconscious mind. Besides talking about your desires, there must be positive action. I certainly do not want you to only be a dreamer. The time has come for action. Saturate your mind with your new found enthusiasm. Make it a full time job. It is not enough, remember, to give this new type of thinking lip service only. Your actions must reflect your new thinking.

If you follow this plan, ideas and solutions to your problems will automatically come to you. You will set into motion the reservoir of knowledge that is lodged in the subconscious level of your mind. It is a well known fact that inventors and creative people agree that many of their ideas just seem to come to them without conscious effort at all times. Once the idea is set into motion, the subconscious mind many times will come up with the solution.

I know a song writer who often gets his hit tunes while he is asleep. His subconscious mind works on the tune while he is asleep. It then comes to him as though he were in a dream. After hearing it in this sort of dream state, he awakens himself and puts the tune down on paper. It is like recording a dream that you want to remember. The utilization of the subconscious in this manner is an integral link in the chain of success.

I can suggest that you do the many things. I can outline a course of action for you, I can expound upon the theories presented in this book to fill twenty volumes, but the course of action must come from you.

The fact that you have expended the time and energy required to digest the material contained in this book is ample evidence that you wish to chart your course toward the attainment of your chosen goal. The canons of attitude and behavior, the principles of mental attitude, the doctrines of social responsibility prescribed by your author can, if rigorously adhered to, constitute your passport to success. You have taken the initial step in the direction of your horizons by seeking out a road map marked with the highways and the detours. Above all, do not put an end to your trip now. At this very moment you are well ahead of the multitudes who, though they may aspire to success, have taken no measures to achieve it. By your diligence you have fortified yourselves with the necessary ammunition to ram down the barriers which stand between you and success. They are stout, formidable obstacles that yield only to the maximum of relentless power. You have that power in your grasp. Use it! There is no greater truth, nor more poignant an observation of wisdom than that embodied in the words of John Greenleaf Whittier: "The saddest words of tongue or pen are these—it might have been."

Do not allow yourself and your conscience to one day be plagued by the grim realization that what might have become your eventual success and the glorious happiness that attends success, was actually thwarted by your own indolence and indifference. You have taken the big step in the right direction; do not go back. There is no turning back where success is concerned. There are thousands of roads which lead to its broad highway, but once you have reached the highway, there are no detours, no short cuts, no trunk lines. It is straight as an arrow, but if you deviate from its course, you will drop off into the deep treacherous ravines of failure and regret that border on each side.

In other words, there are a thousand approaches to the road that ultimately leads to success, but once the approaches have led you to the proper road, you must travel the "straight and narrow" the rest of the way. It is marked along the way with all the milestones which we have previously discussed as "factors to success." Each milestone brings you closer to the goal, and each milestone is charged with a deep and gratifying reward of its own. Eventual success is the sum total of all these rewarding experiences merged into one glorious sensation of achievement.

Let us now assume that we have all enlisted ourselves in the vital project, "Operation Success." We have indi-

cated our first sincere aspirations to effect an achievement of our goal by seeking the enlightenment contained
in this book. We have carefully observed and mentally
digested the methods set forth by the author to chart a
direct, highly efficient course of conduct and philosophy,
to start our journey. This is the food and water needed
along the way to at least offer us insurance against
destruction by thirst and famine. We are eager to as-
semble the gold chain of success by piecing together
each of the many required links. We seek to unite
faith, confidence, perseverance, determination, health
and all the other requisites by diligent application of
each of those success factors. We are convinced that we
must constantly apply the buffer of positive thinking to
keep the links and—once assembled—the success chain,
gleaming and bright and shiny.

We now have a reasonable and logical question. Can
each of us do this by ourselves, by use of our own individual ambition, initiative and eagerness to succeed? It's a
big job. Each of the many required factors has its own
array of problems and obstacles. Each ingredient is itself
fraught with complexities that present obstacles of its
own. These may be some of your thoughts:"I may be
equipped to piece together some of the links, but I may
require guidance to handle the others. I am willing to
apply positive thought all along the way, but there are
still questions which present themselves, little doors to
be opened by keys of additional counselling. There are
no serious impediments, because I believed in all the
principles which the author has set forth for success.

I am convinced that successful accomplishment of my aims is predicated on the solid foundation of positive thinking. But, as with any set of rules pointing the way to the achievement of that for which they were conceived, so with these, there are for the various individuals who wish to apply them, various questions and problems attending the peculiarities of each individual concerned.

As in the case of the hunter, who equipped with all the paraphernalia necessary to bag big game, strayed from the safari to make a prize catch for himself. He had all the knowledge and equipment to kill the on-rushing tiger, but when he pointed the muzzle and his gun jammed, a question quickly presented itself: "What do I do now?" The answer occurred just as quickly as the question, and a split-second later he was rushing back to the safari for help. That's exactly what you are expected to do—enlist help.

There is certainly no disgrace in enlisting aid to achieve what you seek to accomplish. Nor is the glory of achievement in any respect reduced because it required help from others.

Success is rarely accomplished without assistance somewhere along the way. The component elements of society are so interrelated, and so interdependent, that it is difficult, if not impossible, to conceive of a situation wherein the deed of one person does not either directly or indirectly, in some measure, affect another. There is no greater fund of enlightenment than that which results from the exchange of ideas between people. No one person can be a final authority on all matters, and the wise man is quick to recognize that the counsel of others can be of considerable value to himself.

Underlying all of human nature is a distant element of fraternalism which generates in one individual a consideration for the other. Everyone has certain aims, certain goals, desires for achievement, at least an anxiety for survival. This occasions in each, an awareness of the other person, and a realization that there exists a certain dependancy on the other fellow. As a result, each is willing to give something of himself in exchange for something that he may require, whether it be a material thing or an intangible element of information.

This pertains not only to the individual, but to large groups of individuals, corporations, societies, labor organizations, civic bodies, and countless others. The principal purposes of all large conventions is to solicit and effectuate the free exchange of helpful ideas. For the same reason the sales forces will meet on Monday morning, the Kiwanis and the Lions at Tuesday luncheon, the political caucus will convene on a given night, and the labor guild or union will set apart regular meeting periods. These are not meetings brought about for the mere joy of effecting social pleasantries. They are arranged for a very important and concrete purpose—

to exchange ideas, so that one element may obtain from the other something of value, which may be used as an effective implement in the battle for success.

And so should it be with you. Follow the rules, that we have discussed, as the basic and essential factors for success. Practice positive thinking every inch of the way, for without it no amount of help will enable you to reach and maintain the goal you have set up for yourself. But, above all, engage freely with others in the exchange of thoughts and ideas related to your devices for attaining success. The aid that you will receive, in addition to that which you will be able to extend to others, will be of inestimable value. Great stimulation will stem from the inspiration of others, and your own particular efforts will be considerably accelerated to the achievement of your purposes. You have all the equipment, now that you are endowed with the valuable program for success your author has outlined, but you will be amazed to what a degree your tools will be sharpened when subjected to the grindstone of open discussion.

You may, of course, solicit counsel from your author, who is eager to be of assistance at any time you feel compelled to call upon him. But do not fail to supplement this facility with the wonderfully resourceful implement of free discussion and exchange of ideas. Your thoughts will become well-defined and sharply crystallized. Doubts will become resolved into clear cut facts. Questions will find their answers. Devious routes to conviction will become straight and direct paths to decision. There is truly no more stimulating or inspiring an assemblage than that presented by a gathering of mentally-alert, resourceful, positive thinking people. Such a conclave becomes a trading post for ideas and ideals, which will in every respect contribute heavily to your own welfare. You will benefit immeasurably from what you take away with you; you will gain great and enduring gratification from what you are able to contribute to others. Do not deprive yourself of the satisfaction that comes from helping others. It will be returned to you with a remarkable premium. As previously pointed out in an earlier chapter, the attitude of helpfulness and kindness toward your fellow man is just as essential an ingredient of success as any other important factors we have considered.

You may agree with all of the foregoing, but in your mind might exist a question of how to accomplish it. It is not difficult. The art of positive thinking is not a rare or unique human endowment; it is not the exclusive property of a few favored individuals. There are countless positive thinking people in every community, and of these vast numbers many more than you might imagine are eager for the opportunity of discussing their problems and presenting their questions to other positive thinking people or groups. They realize as, I hope, you do, that so much is to be gained from the free exchange and appraisal of their ideas, and a discussion of their problems encountered in the drive to success. They, as you, aspire to accomplish their goals in life, but they require counselling and guidance which will direct their efforts into the most resourceful channels of achievement. They hold a part of the puzzle, you hold the rest of the puzzle. What each of you hold is incomplete and insufficient to spell out a pattern of success. Put them together and you have each contributed heavily toward the construction of a successful project.

It therefore becomes evident that to bring about a circumstance or situation wherein you may seek out those who hold the balance of your puzzle, there remains only the question of how it may be accomplished. The answer is amazingly simple. It contains only one requirement: One person—just one—in any group, circle or community, must be a positive doer, as well as a positive thinker. And what he is asked to do entails no unusual talent, and very little effort and ingenuity. He must only exercise his initiative that is required to convene those who, charged equally with an awareness of the tremendous value attending the discussion and exchange of thoughts and ideas, will welcome the opportunity to meet with others who might hold the key to ultimate success.

As a means of furthering such a project and effecting an accomplishment of the aims to which it is dedicated, the writer is pleased to call your attention to the following facts:

Responsive to numerous requests for suggestions pertinent to the most effective means of making possible the exchange of ideas, discussions, and debate between positive thinking people making their bids for success, your author has been instrumental in the formation of Positive Thinking Groups.

Most successful of all Positive Thinking Groups are those that combine the tested techniques explained in this book with the clinically-proven methods described by Dr. Maxwell Maltz in his revolutionary book, *Psycho-Cybernetics,* which became a best seller.

Dr. Maltz, a brilliant plastic surgeon, had achieved excellent results in correcting bodily disfigurements, facial blemishes and individual features that caused trauma by their deviation from the norm, but he was at a loss to explain a certain percentage of patients whose negative, failure-prone personalities did not alter when the defects, presumably responsible for their inadequate personalities, were removed.

His bafflement led him into lengthy research in scientific disciplines far removed from his specialty. He delved deeply into psychology, psychiatry, physics, physiology and the new science of Cybernetics. He was determined to find out why some patients who had become physically attractive and socially acceptable because of his surgery refused to believe the evidence of their own mirrors.

One of his first clues to their pathetic plight came when he rediscovered the principles of Self-Image psychology which had received scant attention from psychologists since it had been introduced into the literature, posthumously, by the wife of Prescott Lecky, who had originally termed it *Self-Consistency: A Theory of Personality.* Lecky, who taught at Columbia University, had intended it for his doctoral dissertation, but his untimely death brought his work to an end. A number of his colleagues, however, felt his theory was viable and valid, but it received little general attention.

Lecky's theory went a long way toward solving Dr. Maltz's problem, but like Positive Thinking, in itself, it did not ensure uniform results. Egos buffeted by years of self-depreciation and despair made it difficult for individuals to think of themselves as popular, positive and successful. These years of thinking of themselves as ugly and doomed to fail had produced a conditioned reflex seemingly impossible to overcome.

It was at this point that Norbert Weiner, a mathematical genius who was chairman of the department in his specialty at M.I.T., published *Cybernetics,* a methodology which guaranteed the success of mechanical systems and brought out the many analogies between computers and man's brain. By synthesizing Lecky's Self-Consistency theory, now termed Self-Image psychology, Cybernetics and Pavlovian Reflexology (so-called after Dr. Ivan Pavlov, the great Russian physiologist), Dr. Maltz now had his answer for those whose personalities did not change to complement their altered appearance. His psychological failures reached the vanishing point, and the entire process is revealed in his book which is already a classic.

The big breakthrough came in Cybernetics when he learned that the human brain, like the computer, if programmed correctly, is a goal-oriented and goal-directed servomechanism that cannot fail if man is motivated to succeed, no matter how difficult the goal. Just as the missile, which Dr. Wiener had in mind, can unerringly seek out its target, correcting its flight path on the way, man, too, can utilize positive and negative feedback to keep him on his course. The theory, proven many times, is radically changing the mystique of self-improvement books.

There is no space here to go into detail about this remarkable and consistent method of changing an inadequate personality, but *Psycho-Cybernetics* may be purchased from the Wilshire Book Company. Thousands of letters from readers indicate it may be the most important book you may ever read.

Because of many requests from readers who wish to exchange ideas about the progress they have made by concentrated study of *Psycho-Cybernetics,* the writer is pleased to announce he has acted to form study groups from coast to coast. This has been done so that you may benefit from different methods of approach developed by members who have already made vast changes in their lives.

If you write me, I shall make every effort to find you a convenient study group to enhance your understanding of this new science.

There are no dues, initiation fees or obligation of any sort for joining these groups, and the writer has taken on the responsibility because he firmly believes two heads (or any number you choose) are better than one. You will be mingling with individuals whose hopes and aspirations are similar to your own. Many groups which discuss the courses of action recommended in *Psycho-Cybernetics* are already in operation, and familiarizing yourself with its contents is a necessity.

To ascertain the closest group and also purchase the book, it is necessary only to send your name, address and telephone number, along with a self-addressed envelope (and *$2.30* if you have not yet read the book *Psycho-Cybernetics*) to Melvin Powers, Wilshire Book Company 12015 Sherman Road, No. Hollywood, California 91605.

I am confident it will be the biggest step toward self-improvement you will ever take. By all means, do it today and good wishes for your success.

SUCCESS

Success is in the way you walk the
    paths of life each day;
It's in the little things you do and in
    the things you say.
Success is not in getting rich or rising
    high to fame;
It's not alone in winning goals which
    all men hope to claim.
Success is being big of heart and clean
    and broad of mind.
It's being faithful to your friends and,
    to the stranger, kind.
It's in the children whom you love
    and all they learn from you;
Success depends on character and
    everything you do.

A PERSONAL WORD FROM MELVIN POWERS
PUBLISHER, WILSHIRE BOOK COMPANY

Dear Friend:

My goal is to publish interesting, informative, and inspirational books. You can help me accomplish this by answering the following questions, either by phone or by mail. Or, if convenient for you, I would welcome the opportunity to visit with you in my office and hear your comments in person.

Did you enjoy reading this book? Why?

Would you enjoy reading another similar book?

What idea in the book impressed you the most?

If applicable to your situation, have you incorporated this idea in your daily life?

Is there a chapter that could serve as a theme for an entire book? Please explain.

If you have an idea for a book, I would welcome discussing it with you. If you already have one in progress, write or call me concerning possible publication. I can be reached at (213) 875-1711 or (213) 983-1105.

Sincerely yours,
MELVIN POWERS

12015 Sherman Road
North Hollywood, California 91605

MELVIN POWERS SELF-IMPROVEMENT LIBRARY

ASTROLOGY

ASTROLOGY: A FASCINATING HISTORY *P. Naylor*	2.00
ASTROLOGY: HOW TO CHART YOUR HOROSCOPE *Max Heindel*	3.00
ASTROLOGY: YOUR PERSONAL SUN-SIGN GUIDE *Beatrice Ryder*	3.00
ASTROLOGY FOR EVERYDAY LIVING *Janet Harris*	2.00
ASTROLOGY MADE EASY *Astarte*	3.00
ASTROLOGY MADE PRACTICAL *Alexandra Kayhle*	3.00
ASTROLOGY, ROMANCE, YOU AND THE STARS *Anthony Norvell*	4.00
MY WORLD OF ASTROLOGY *Sydney Omarr*	4.00
THOUGHT DIAL *Sydney Omarr*	3.00
ZODIAC REVEALED *Rupert Gleadow*	2.00

BRIDGE

BRIDGE BIDDING MADE EASY *Edwin B. Kantar*	5.00
BRIDGE CONVENTIONS *Edwin B. Kantar*	4.00
BRIDGE HUMOR *Edwin B. Kantar*	3.00
COMPETITIVE BIDDING IN MODERN BRIDGE *Edgar Kaplan*	4.00
DEFENSIVE BRIDGE PLAY COMPLETE *Edwin B. Kantar*	10.00
HOW TO IMPROVE YOUR BRIDGE *Alfred Sheinwold*	2.00
INTRODUCTION TO DEFENDER'S PLAY *Edwin B. Kantar*	3.00
SHORT CUT TO WINNING BRIDGE *Alfred Sheinwold*	3.00
TEST YOUR BRIDGE PLAY *Edwin B. Kantar*	3.00
WINNING DECLARER PLAY *Dorothy Hayden Truscott*	4.00

BUSINESS, STUDY & REFERENCE

CONVERSATION MADE EASY *Elliot Russell*	2.00
EXAM SECRET *Dennis B. Jackson*	2.00
FIX-IT BOOK *Arthur Symons*	2.00
HOW TO DEVELOP A BETTER SPEAKING VOICE *M. Hellier*	2.00
HOW TO MAKE A FORTUNE IN REAL ESTATE *Albert Winnikoff*	3.00
INCREASE YOUR LEARNING POWER *Geoffrey A. Dudley*	2.00
MAGIC OF NUMBERS *Robert Tocquet*	2.00
PRACTICAL GUIDE TO BETTER CONCENTRATION *Melvin Powers*	2.00
PRACTICAL GUIDE TO PUBLIC SPEAKING *Maurice Forley*	3.00
7 DAYS TO FASTER READING *William S. Schaill*	3.00
SONGWRITERS RHYMING DICTIONARY *Jane Shaw Whitfield*	5.00
SPELLING MADE EASY *Lester D. Basch & Dr. Milton Finkelstein*	2.00
STUDENT'S GUIDE TO BETTER GRADES *J. A. Rickard*	2.00
TEST YOURSELF—Find Your Hidden Talent *Jack Shafer*	2.00
YOUR WILL & WHAT TO DO ABOUT IT *Attorney Samuel G. Kling*	3.00

CALLIGRAPHY

CALLIGRAPHY—The Art of Beautfiul Writing *Katherine Jeffares*	5.00

CHESS & CHECKERS

BEGINNER'S GUIDE TO WINNING CHESS *Fred Reinfeld*	3.00
BETTER CHESS—How to Play *Fred Reinfeld*	2.00
CHECKERS MADE EASY *Tom Wiswell*	2.00
CHESS IN TEN EASY LESSONS *Larry Evans*	3.00
CHESS MADE EASY *Milton L. Hanauer*	3.00
CHESS MASTERY—A New Approach *Fred Reinfeld*	2.00
CHESS PROBLEMS FOR BEGINNERS *edited by Fred Reinfeld*	2.00
CHESS SECRETS REVEALED *Fred Reinfeld*	2.00
CHESS STRATEGY—An Expert's Guide *Fred Reinfeld*	2.00
CHESS TACTICS FOR BEGINNERS *edited by Fred Reinfeld*	2.00
CHESS THEORY & PRACTICE *Morry & Mitchell*	2.00
HOW TO WIN AT CHECKERS *Fred Reinfeld*	2.00
1001 BRILLIANT WAYS TO CHECKMATE *Fred Reinfeld*	3.00
1001 WINNING CHESS SACRIFICES & COMBINATIONS *Fred Reinfeld*	3.00
SOVIET CHESS *Edited by R. G. Wade*	3.00

COOKERY & HERBS

CULPEPER'S HERBAL REMEDIES *Dr. Nicholas Culpeper*	2.00
FAST GOURMET COOKBOOK *Poppy Cannon*	2.50

_____ HEALING POWER OF HERBS *May Bethel*   3.00
_____ HEALING POWER OF NATURAL FOODS *May Bethel*   3.00
_____ HERB HANDBOOK *Dawn MacLeod*   3.00
_____ HERBS FOR COOKING AND HEALING *Dr. Donald Law*   2.00
_____ HERBS FOR HEALTH—How to Grow & Use Them *Louise Evans Doole*   2.00
_____ HOME GARDEN COOKBOOK—Delicious Natural Food Recipes *Ken Kraft*   3.00
_____ MEDICAL HERBALIST *edited by Dr. J. R. Yemm*   3.00
_____ NATURAL FOOD COOKBOOK *Dr. Harry C. Bond*   3.00
_____ NATURE'S MEDICINES *Richard Lucas*   3.00
_____ VEGETABLE GARDENING FOR BEGINNERS *Hugh Wiberg*   2.00
_____ VEGETABLES FOR TODAY'S GARDENS *R. Milton Carleton*   2.00
_____ VEGETARIAN COOKERY *Janet Walker*   3.00
_____ VEGETARIAN COOKING MADE EASY & DELECTABLE *Veronica Vezza*   2.00
_____ VEGETARIAN DELIGHTS—A Happy Cookbook for Health *K. R. Mehta*   2.00
_____ VEGETARIAN GOURMET COOKBOOK *Joyce McKinnel*   3.00

GAMBLING & POKER

_____ ADVANCED POKER STRATEGY & WINNING PLAY *A. D. Livingston*   3.00
_____ HOW NOT TO LOSE AT POKER *Jeffrey Lloyd Castle*   3.00
_____ HOW TO WIN AT DICE GAMES *Skip Frey*   3.00
_____ HOW TO WIN AT POKER *Terence Reese & Anthony T. Watkins*   2.00
_____ SECRETS OF WINNING POKER *George S. Coffin*   3.00
_____ WINNING AT CRAPS *Dr. Lloyd T. Commins*   2.00
_____ WINNING AT GIN *Chester Wander & Cy Rice*   3.00
_____ WINNING AT POKER—An Expert's Guide *John Archer*   3.00
_____ WINNING AT 21—An Expert's Guide *John Archer*   3.00
_____ WINNING POKER SYSTEMS *Norman Zadeh*   3.00

HEALTH

_____ DR. LINDNER'S SPECIAL WEIGHT CONTROL METHOD   1.50
_____ HELP YOURSELF TO BETTER SIGHT *Margaret Darst Corbett*   3.00
_____ HOW TO IMPROVE YOUR VISION *Dr. Robert A. Kraskin*   2.00
_____ HOW YOU CAN STOP SMOKING PERMANENTLY *Ernest Caldwell*   2.00
_____ MIND OVER PLATTER *Peter G. Lindner, M.D.*   2.00
_____ NATURE'S WAY TO NUTRITION & VIBRANT HEALTH *Robert J. Scrutton*   3.00
_____ NEW CARBOHYDRATE DIET COUNTER *Patti Lopez-Pereira*   1.50
_____ PSYCHEDELIC ECSTASY *William Marshall & Gilbert W. Taylor*   2.00
_____ REFLEXOLOGY *Dr. Maybelle Segal*   2.00
_____ YOU CAN LEARN TO RELAX *Dr. Samuel Gutwirth*   2.00
_____ YOUR ALLERGY—What To Do About It *Allan Knight, M.D.*   3.00

HOBBIES

_____ BEACHCOMBING FOR BEGINNERS *Norman Hickin*   2.00
_____ BLACKSTONE'S MODERN CARD TRICKS *Harry Blackstone*   3.00
_____ BLACKSTONE'S SECRETS OF MAGIC *Harry Blackstone*   2.00
_____ BUTTERFLIES   2.50
_____ COIN COLLECTING FOR BEGINNERS *Burton Hobson & Fred Reinfeld*   2.00
_____ ENTERTAINING WITH ESP *Tony 'Doc' Shiels*   2.00
_____ 400 FASCINATING MAGIC TRICKS YOU CAN DO *Howard Thurston*   3.00
_____ GOULD'S GOLD & SILVER GUIDE TO COINS *Maurice Gould*   2.00
_____ HOW I TURN JUNK INTO FUN AND PROFIT *Sari*   3.00
_____ HOW TO PLAY THE HARMONICA FOR FUN AND PROFIT *Hal Leighton*   3.00
_____ HOW TO WRITE A HIT SONG & SELL IT *Tommy Boyce*   7.00
_____ JUGGLING MADE EASY *Rudolf Dittrich*   2.00
_____ MAGIC MADE EASY *Byron Wels*   2.00
_____ STAMP COLLECTING FOR BEGINNERS *Burton Hobson*   2.00
_____ STAMP COLLECTING FOR FUN & PROFIT *Frank Cetin*   2.00

HORSE PLAYERS' WINNING GUIDES

_____ BETTING HORSES TO WIN *Les Conklin*   3.00
_____ ELIMINATE THE LOSERS *Bob McKnight*   3.00
_____ HOW TO PICK WINNING HORSES *Bob McKnight*   3.00
_____ HOW TO WIN AT THE RACES *Sam (The Genius) Lewin*   3.00
_____ HOW YOU CAN BEAT THE RACES *Jack Kavanagh*   3.00

____MAGIC IN YOUR MIND *U. S. Andersen*		4.00
____MAGIC OF THINKING BIG *Dr. David J. Schwartz*		3.00
____MAGIC POWER OF YOUR MIND *Walter M. Germain*		4.00
____MENTAL POWER THROUGH SLEEP SUGGESTION *Melvin Powers*		2.00
____NEW GUIDE TO RATIONAL LIVING *Albert Ellis, Ph.D. & R. Harper, Ph.D.*		3.00
____OUR TROUBLED SELVES *Dr. Allan Fromme*		3.00
____PRACTICAL GUIDE TO SUCCESS & POPULARITY *C. W. Bailey*		2.00
____PSYCHO-CYBERNETICS *Maxwell Maltz, M.D.*		2.00
____SCIENCE OF MIND IN DAILY LIVING *Dr. Donald Curtis*		3.00
____SECRET POWER OF THE PYRAMIDS *U. S. Andersen*		4.00
____SECRET OF SECRETS *U. S. Andersen*		4.00
____STUTTERING AND WHAT YOU CAN DO ABOUT IT *W. Johnson, Ph.D.*		2.50
____SUCCESS-CYBERNETICS *U. S. Andersen*		4.00
____10 DAYS TO A GREAT NEW LIFE *William E. Edwards*		3.00
____THINK AND GROW RICH *Napoleon Hill*		3.00
____**THREE MAGIC WORDS** *U. S. Andersen*		4.00
____TREASURY OF THE ART OF LIVING *Sidney S. Greenberg*		5.00
____YOU ARE NOT THE TARGET *Laura Huxley*		3.00
____YOUR SUBCONSCIOUS POWER *Charles M. Simmons*		4.00
____YOUR THOUGHTS CAN CHANGE YOUR LIFE *Dr. Donald Curtis*		3.00

SPORTS

____ARCHERY—An Expert's Guide *Dan Stamp*		2.00
____BICYCLING FOR FUN AND GOOD HEALTH *Kenneth E. Luther*		2.00
____BILLIARDS—Pocket • Carom • Three Cushion *Clive Cottingham, Jr.*		2.00
____CAMPING-OUT 101 Ideas & Activities *Bruno Knobel*		2.00
____COMPLETE GUIDE TO FISHING *Vlad Evanoff*		2.00
____HOW TO WIN AT POCKET BILLIARDS *Edward D. Knuchell*		3.00
____LEARNING & TEACHING SOCCER SKILLS *Eric Worthington*		3.00
____MOTORCYCLING FOR BEGINNERS *I. G. Edmonds*		2.00
____PRACTICAL BOATING *W. S. Kals*		3.00
____RACQUETBALL MADE EASY *Steve Lubarsky, Rod Delson & Jack Scagnetti*		3.00
____SECRET OF BOWLING STRIKES *Dawson Taylor*		3.00
____SECRET OF PERFECT PUTTING *Horton Smith & Dawson Taylor*		3.00
____SECRET WHY FISH BITE *James Westman*		2.00
____SOCCER—The game & how to play it *Gary Rosenthal*		2.00
____STARTING SOCCER *Edward F. Dolan, Jr.*		2.00
____TABLE TENNIS MADE EASY *Johnny Leach*		2.00

TENNIS LOVERS' LIBRARY

____BEGINNER'S GUIDE TO WINNING TENNIS *Helen Hull Jacobs*		2.00
____HOW TO BEAT BETTER TENNIS PLAYERS *Loring Fiske*		4.00
____HOW TO IMPROVE YOUR TENNIS—Style, Strategy & Analysis *C. Wilson*		2.00
____INSIDE TENNIS—Techniques of Winning *Jim Leighton*		3.00
____PLAY TENNIS WITH ROSEWALL *Ken Rosewall*		2.00
____PSYCH YOURSELF TO BETTER TENNIS *Dr. Walter A. Luszki*		2.00
____SUCCESSFUL TENNIS *Neale Fraser*		2.00
____TENNIS FOR BEGINNERS *Dr. H. A. Murray*		2.00
____TENNIS MADE EASY *Joel Brecheen*		2.00
____WEEKEND TENNIS—How to have fun & win at the same time *Bill Talbert*		3.00
____WINNING WITH PERCENTAGE TENNIS—Smart Strategy *Jack Lowe*		2.00

WILSHIRE PET LIBRARY

____DOG OBEDIENCE TRAINING *Gust Kessopulos*		3.00
____DOG TRAINING MADE EASY & FUN *John W. Kellogg*		2.00
____HOW TO BRING UP YOUR PET DOG *Kurt Unkelbach*		2.00
____HOW TO RAISE & TRAIN YOUR PUPPY *Jeff Griffen*		2.00
____PIGEONS: HOW TO RAISE & TRAIN THEM *William H. Allen, Jr.*		2.00

The books listed above can be obtained from your book dealer or directly from Melvin Powers. When ordering, please remit 30¢ per book postage & handling. Send for our free illustrated catalog of self-improvement books.

Melvin Powers
12015 Sherman Road, No. Hollywood, California 91605

WILSHIRE HORSE LOVERS' LIBRARY

____AMATEUR HORSE BREEDER *A. C. Leighton Hardman*	3.00
____AMERICAN QUARTER HORSE IN PICTURES *Margaret Cabell Self*	3.00
____APPALOOSA HORSE *Donna & Bill Richardson*	3.00
____ARABIAN HORSE *Reginald S. Summerhays*	2.00
____ART OF WESTERN RIDING *Suzanne Norton Jones*	3.00
____AT THE HORSE SHOW *Margaret Cabell Self*	3.00
____BACK-YARD FOAL *Peggy Jett Pittinger*	3.00
____BACK-YARD HORSE *Peggy Jett Pittinger*	3.00
____BASIC DRESSAGE *Jean Froissard*	2.00
____BEGINNER'S GUIDE TO HORSEBACK RIDING *Sheila Wall*	2.00
____BEGINNER'S GUIDE TO THE WESTERN HORSE *Natlee Kenoyer*	2.00
____BITS—THEIR HISTORY, USE AND MISUSE *Louis Taylor*	3.00
____BREAKING & TRAINING THE DRIVING HORSE *Doris Ganton*	2.00
____BREAKING YOUR HORSE'S BAD HABITS *W. Dayton Sumner*	3.00
____CAVALRY MANUAL OF HORSEMANSHIP *Gordon Wright*	3.00
____COMPLETE TRAINING OF HORSE AND RIDER *Colonel Alois Podhajsky*	4.00
____DISORDERS OF THE HORSE & WHAT TO DO ABOUT THEM *E. Hanauer*	2.00
____DOG TRAINING MADE EASY & FUN *John W. Kellogg*	2.00
____DRESSAGE—A Study of the Finer Points in Riding *Henry Wynmalen*	4.00
____DRIVING HORSES *Sallie Walrond*	2.00
____ENDURANCE RIDING *Ann Hyland*	2.00
____EQUITATION *Jean Froissard*	4.00
____FIRST AID FOR HORSES *Dr. Charles H. Denning, Jr.*	2.00
____FUN OF RAISING A COLT *Rubye & Frank Griffith*	3.00
____FUN ON HORSEBACK *Margaret Cabell Self*	4.00
____GYMKHANA GAMES *Natlee Kenoyer*	2.00
____HORSE DISEASES—Causes, Symptoms & Treatment *Dr. H. G. Belschner*	3.00
____HORSE OWNER'S CONCISE GUIDE *Elsie V. Hanauer*	2.00
____HORSE SELECTION & CARE FOR BEGINNERS *George H. Conn*	3.00
____HORSE SENSE—A complete guide to riding and care *Alan Deacon*	4.00
____HORSEBACK RIDING FOR BEGINNERS *Louis Taylor*	4.00
____HORSEBACK RIDING MADE EASY & FUN *Sue Henderson Coen*	3.00
____HORSES—Their Selection, Care & Handling *Margaret Cabell Self*	3.00
____HOW TO BUY A BETTER HORSE & SELL THE HORSE YOU OWN	3.00
____HOW TO ENJOY YOUR QUARTER HORSE *Williard H. Porter*	3.00
____HUNTER IN PICTURES *Margaret Cabell Self*	2.00
____ILLUSTRATED BOOK OF THE HORSE *S. Sidney* (8½" x 11½")	10.00
____ILLUSTRATED HORSE MANAGEMENT—400 Illustrations *Dr. E. Mayhew*	6.00
____ILLUSTRATED HORSE TRAINING *Captain M. H. Hayes*	5.00
____ILLUSTRATED HORSEBACK RIDING FOR BEGINNERS *Jeanne Mellin*	2.00
____JUMPING—Learning & Teaching *Jean Froissard*	3.00
____KNOW ALL ABOUT HORSES *Harry Disston*	3.00
____LAME HORSE—Causes, Symptoms & Treatment *Dr. James R. Rooney*	3.00
____LAW & YOUR HORSE *Edward H. Greene*	3.00
____LIPIZZANERS & THE SPANISH RIDING SCHOOL *W. Reuter* (4¼" x 6")	2.50
____MANUAL OF HORSEMANSHIP *Harold Black*	5.0C
____MORGAN HORSE IN PICTURES *Margaret Cabell Self*	2.00
____MOVIE HORSES—The Fascinating Techniques of Training *Anthony Amaral*	2.00
____POLICE HORSES *Judith Campbell*	2.00
____PRACTICAL GUIDE TO HORSESHOEING	3.00
____PRACTICAL GUIDE TO OWNING YOUR OWN HORSE *Steven D. Price*	2.00
____PRACTICAL HORSE PSYCHOLOGY *Moyra Williams*	3.00
____PROBLEM HORSES Guide for Curing Serious Behavior Habits *Summerhays*	2.00
____REINSMAN OF THE WEST—BRIDLES & BITS *Ed Connell*	4.00
____RESCHOOLING THE THOROUGHBRED *Peggy Jett Pittenger*	3.00
____RIDE WESTERN *Louis Taylor*	3.00
____SCHOOLING YOUR YOUNG HORSE *George Wheatley*	2.00
____STABLE MANAGEMENT FOR THE OWNER-GROOM *George Wheatley*	4.00
____STALLION MANAGEMENT—A Guide for Stud Owners *A. C. Hardman*	3.00
____TEACHING YOUR HORSE TO JUMP *W. J. Froud*	2.00
____TRAIL HORSES & TRAIL RIDING *Anne & Perry Westbrook*	2.00
____TRAINING YOUR HORSE TO SHOW *Neale Haley*	3.00
____TREATING COMMON DISEASES OF YOUR HORSE *Dr. George H. Conn*	3.00
____TREATING HORSE AILMENTS *G. W. Serth*	2.00
____WESTERN HORSEBACK RIDING *Glen Balch*	3.00
____WONDERFUL WORLD OF PONIES *Peggy Jett Pittenger* (8½" x 11½")	4.00
____YOU AND YOUR PONY *Pepper Mainwaring Healey* (8½" x 11")	6.00
____YOUR FIRST HORSE *George C. Saunders, M.D.*	3.00
____YOUR PONY BOOK *Hermann Wiederhold*	2.00
____YOUR WESTERN HORSE *Nelson C. Nye*	2.00

The books listed above can be obtained from your book dealer or directly from Melvin Powers. When ordering, please remit 30¢ per book postage & handling. Send for our free illustrated catalog of self-improvement books.

Melvin Powers

12015 Sherman Road, No. Hollywood, California 91605

NOTES

NOTES

NOTES

NOTES

NOTES

NOTES